A Mom's Guide
to making memories last

simple, inexpensive ways
to scrapbook and journal

Crystal Bowman

Revell
Grand Rapids, Michigan

© 2006 by Crystal Bowman

Published by Fleming H. Revell
a division of Baker Publishing Group
P.O. Box 6287, Grand Rapids, MI 49516-6287
www.revellbooks.com

Printed in the United States of America

Library of Congress Cataloging-in-Publication Data
Bowman, Crystal.
    A mom's guide to making memories last : simple, inexpensive ways to scrapbook and journal / Crystal Bowman.
       p.   cm.
    Includes bibliographical references and index.
    ISBN 0-8007-3081-X (pbk.)
      1. Mother and child—Religious aspects—Christianity.
    2. Scrapbook journaling. 3. Scrapbooks. I. Title
    BV4529.18.B69 2006
    248.8'431—dc22   2005026359

The ideas for scrapbooking and journaling in this book are not medical or health advice. Readers are reminded to seek professional help for diagnosis and treatment of emotional and mental issues.

Her children arise and call her blessed.

Proverbs 31:28

contents

Sweet Dreams and Carefree Days   9
Capture the Memories to Build the Future

1. Books That Mothers Write   13
   Journaling for Your Children
2. Celebrate throughout the Year   51
   Holiday Journals, Traditions, and Family Rituals
3. Keep the Adventures   83
   Family Vacations and Special Events
4. Just for You   97
   Personal and Spiritual Journaling
5. "Thanks for the Memories, Mom"   127
   Creative Ideas That Leave a Legacy of Love

Build the Future   153
Motherhood Is a Ministry

Notes   155
Index   157

sweet dreams
and carefree days

Capture the Memories to Build the Future

When people ask my friend Sharon, who has six children, "How do you do it all?" she replies, "I don't."

She explains: "There are kids who have extravagant birthday parties and invite the whole class plus the neighbors, and many kids are involved in two or three different sports. My kids celebrate their birthdays with their siblings, because I have to give six birthday parties each year, and my children are allowed to choose one sport. I don't do it all, because I can't do it all."

Sharon is a wise mother, because she's focused on the obvious but oft-forgotten key to motherhood: recognizing what's realistic for the family and finding a way to make the most of that, despite what society insists we must incorporate into our lives.

Life is about choices, and we can choose, to a certain extent, what kind of mothers to be—and what kind of memories to give our children. Obviously, we can't control everything that happens to our children or our families. Nobody chooses sickness or war or terrorism. You wouldn't choose a terrible accident. Who would ever choose to lose a job or move away from a place he or she loves? While these things may not be our choice, memories of them become a part of our children's lives because of the world we live in.

Moms, however, have many opportunities to override the disappointment, pain, and horror in this world. As moms, we can create pleasant memories for our children. From kitty-cat pancakes in the morning to choo-choo train stories at bedtime, the daily routines we establish become memories our children can enjoy for the rest of their lives. Holidays, vacations, and family activities add to childhood memories and give our children the foundation—a sense of safety, belonging, and confidence—they need to become emotionally healthy adults.

This book is about creating memories for your children and also about preserving them. It's about looking for inventive ways to save and pass along the treasured moments our brains couldn't possibly retain without little triggers like pictures, stories, and keepsakes. I've been journaling for my now-adult children since they were toddlers; as I read through their journals, I'm amazed at how much I would have forgotten if I hadn't written it down.

Preserving memories for our children is a great idea, but it isn't an idea for which I can take credit. It's an idea that goes back centuries, to the beginning of time. Chapters three and four of the book of Joshua give the dramatic account of how the Israelites crossed the Jordan River. After the crossing, God told Joshua to build a memorial of stones at the place where the people would camp that night. In obedience, Joshua instructed the people to choose twelve men—one from each tribe—to take a stone from the middle of the Jordan and bring it to camp.

There was a beautiful purpose in building this monument of stones—to preserve the memory of this amazing experience. Look at what Joshua 4:20–24 records:

> And Joshua set up at Gilgal the twelve stones they had taken out of the Jordan. He said to the Israelites, "In the future when your descendants ask their fathers, 'What do these stones mean?' tell them, 'Israel crossed the Jordan on dry ground.' For the LORD your God dried up the Jordan before you until you had crossed over. The LORD your God did to the Jordan just what he had done to the Red Sea when he dried it up before us until we had crossed over. He did this so that all the peoples of the earth might know that the hand of the LORD is powerful and so that you might always fear the LORD your God.

The stones would remain a memorial to the people of Israel forever, a memorial of how God delivered them from sinking in deep waters, a memorial for long after the people were gone and their footprints were washed away by the Jordan's waters.

God wants us to tell our children about our lives and the lives of our ancestors. He wants to remind them of his faithfulness and his blessings so they'll continue to love and serve him. Psalm 78:2–4 says, "I will utter . . . what we have heard and known, what our fathers have told us. We will not hide them from their children; we will tell the next generation the praiseworthy deeds of the LORD, his power, and the wonders he has done."

Preserving memories for our children is a way to pass the baton of faith from one generation to the next. When we record what God has done in the lives of our loved ones, they'll be reminded over and over again that we serve a mighty and living God.

Making and preserving wonderful memories for your family doesn't have to be difficult, time-consuming, expensive, or boring. As you open the pages of this book, you'll discover many fun, easy, and affordable ways to create and preserve treasured moments. There's a wide variety of ideas, tips, and techniques presented in these sections for moms with all kinds of different personalities, affinities, skills, and situations. Some ideas or tips may be more challenging, but most are very simple and doable with what you have and where you are. Choose what works best for you, considering your schedule, interests, and even your kids' personalities.

I once saw a bumper sticker that said, "A Happy Childhood Lasts a Lifetime."

The even greater truth is that you can create a happy childhood for your children by living out your mom responsibilities as a ministry—and leaving a legacy of the good thoughts, times, and events in your lives for the next generation.

Just ask my friend Sharon.

Better yet, ask her kids.

1

books that mothers write

Journaling for Your Children

A picture is worth a thousand words, but not everything can be captured in a picture. Your children are saying and doing things they'll want to remember, and your family is experiencing things you'll all want to remember.

But if the thought of journaling raises your blood pressure or causes you to break out in hives, read on! You need not be an English major or be enrolled in memoir-writing classes to keep a journal. Recording thoughts, feelings, events, and milestones can be simpler and less consuming than you think. Grab a pen or pencil—even a crayon or marker will do. You're about to learn some fun and easy ways to write journals your children will cherish forever.

Your Book
of
Quotes

Be sure to record the age of your child and the date. Perhaps even the place or circumstance. Once you get your confidence for journaling by keeping a book of quotes (I can just hear you saying, "I can do this!"), think about jotting down the rest of the story.

- How did you or others react?
- What inspired the events?
- What were you thinking or feeling about what your child said—either at the time or afterward?

out of the mouths of babes

I started writing for my son Rob when he was two years old because I wanted to remember the funny things he said. His journal actually started out as simply a quote book. You know, a cute thing he said here or an amazing insight he uttered there. Here's an example:

> I was having trouble getting the child-proof cap off your bottle of vitamins. As you watched me struggle, you offered some pretty wise advice for a two-year-old: "Read the directions, Mommy!" (May 20, 1980).

As Rob grew I continued writing down those cute, funny phrases, but I also wrote about his activities and special moments. That's when his book became a journal. I began journaling for my son Scott and my daughter, Teri, when they were around two years of age also.

See how easy this can be? When the baby book ends, the journal begins!

keep it simple!

For each of my three children, I purchased a thick six-by-eleven-inch spiral notebook. I covered the journals with leftover wallpaper from their bedrooms to give them a personal touch. I write in ink and do not have the penmanship of a calligrapher.

Remember, moms, this is not the time to be a perfectionist. Keep in mind that your goal is to preserve memories, not to win an award or to get published. Unless you are Anne Frank or Jim Elliot, your journals probably won't get published. Still, they could change lives.

tips for beginners

If you're not a journaler by nature and wonder where to even start, try this and watch your words flow: jot down just one notable thing

Intimidation Stoppers

Paper Picks: You can buy an expensive journal if it inspires you, but spiral notebooks work just as well and cost anywhere from fifty cents to a couple dollars at the grocery or department store.

On Your Mark: Too afraid to write because you fear generations to come will see only jumbled thoughts or your messy penmanship? Or maybe you're just afraid of making a mistake with that ink pen in your nice notebook, scrapbook, or journal. No problem. Use a pencil. Or better yet—erasable ink pens give you the brightness of ink on the page and a way to fix mistakes as you go.

Write or Wrong? Remind yourself that rushed scrawl or imperfection is actually a valuable reminder of your presence. A tiny flaw or the flair of your handwriting leaves a physical impression that "a real human being was here." All the little ink blots or scribbles show that you cared enough in the busyness of your days to keep a record of what really matters regardless of time and space—your relationships. That's a message words alone may not convey.

on any given day. Don't worry about writing down long entries every single day or fear you're not logging enough detail.

Simply begin with one moment in your child's life, then write a few sentences. Keep the entries short and sweet. There's no need to be wordy or overly emotional. Watch as the simple things you jot down begin to build. All the small things you've noted over time can quickly add up to a picture of your child's life—and yours.

journal like you're writing a letter

Start by writing down the date. Maybe add the time and place. Now tell one thing that happened on that day. Did you just spend an hour reading and playing? What books did you pick? What games did you play? Think what you would say if you were telling someone far away about what this hour was like—the simple things, like what you did (or didn't do). For example, you might say, "We took a nap together, wrapped in Nana's quilt, the blue and white one given to us when you were born."

Think of how fun it is years later to read about the ordinary moments of a week. It's like imaginary time travel—you get to walk with someone through his or her days, only the recorded events really happened!

Here are some excerpts from my kids' journals:

In Rob's Journal

November 4, 1980—It is election day today. I went to cast my vote for the next president of the United States. I brought you with me, and you were very patient as we waited in line. On the way back home, you asked me, "Now that we voted, are we married?"

October 14, 1982—Dad called from work to say hi and see how we were doing, so I let you talk to him for a few minutes. When you were talking to him, you asked, "Hey, Dad, if I spit into the phone, will your ear get wet?"

June 15, 1983—You were very annoyed by the fact that Scott was jumping on your bed. You told him repeatedly to stop, but he kept on jumping. After much frustration you finally tried a different approach. In a very authoritative voice, you commanded, "Children, obey your brother in the Lord, for this is right!"

February 10, 1997—It was your turn to set the table today, so I asked you to please put ice in the glasses. You replied, "Sure. It's a cold job, but somebody has to do it!"

In Scott's Journal

April 4, 1984—It was bedtime and I was exhausted. After our usual bedtime routine, I finally said, "No more storybooks and no more talking. It's time to be quiet and go to sleep." You were quiet for a few minutes, then said, "But, Mom, I have a very, very, very important question." "Okay," I replied. "What is it?" Then you asked me your very, very, very important question: "Is *booger brain* a bad word?"

December 12, 1984—I came home from the hospital yesterday with your new baby sister. You watched me change her diaper and were amazed at how tiny she was. When you looked at her tummy, you asked, "When is her extension cord going to come off?"

April 12, 1985—Today is Easter Sunday. We put on our Sunday best and went to church. After Sunday school I asked you what your story was about. You replied, "Oh, you know, when Jesus came out of the tube."

March 14, 1986—We drove to Chicago's O'Hare airport and planned on flying to Salt Lake City, Utah, for a few days of skiing, but we were stranded at the airport due to bad weather. After several long, tiresome hours of waiting, you asked, "When are we ever going to get to U-Haul?"

In Teri's Journal

November 20, 1987—I was helping you go to the bathroom, when you heard your brothers nearby. You got very upset and said, "Mom, shut the door! I don't want the boys to see my privacy!"

July 31, 1988—Your cousin Jamie stayed overnight because Aunt Glenda just had another baby. You and Jamie were playing downstairs with Scott, and then you came upstairs to get a drink. "How is Jamie doing?" I asked. You replied, "She's playing happily ever after."

A Mom's Guide to Making Memories Last

September 19, 1990—I set a bowl of peas in front of you on the dinner table. You took one look at them and said, "I'm not going to eat those. That's just broccoli, only you made it in balls."

November 21, 1991—You wanted to wear your Mayflower Preschool sweatshirt to school today. I tried to talk you out of it, since I was sure the other first-graders would tease you. Since you insisted on wearing it, I agreed, but I worried about you all day. When you returned home from school, I asked if the kids said anything about your sweatshirt. "No," you replied. "No one else can read yet."

use your calendar

I don't write in my kids' journals every day. I don't even write in them every week. When something happens that's journal material, I just jot a note on my calendar on the day it occurs. Then, when I have time to write or am more in the mood, I sit down with the journals and my calendar and get caught up. I've found that writing in all three of my kids' journals at once is more time efficient—I can get in the mood and carve out a little more time to get down the things I want to say.

pinpoint what's special

So what exactly is journal worthy? It's up to you to decide this. It can be anything that's funny or amazing or that marks a place in life where changes occur. An easy starting point is to record what happens at milestone moments like the following.

School—The Big First Day

Capture the excitement and novelty of the first day of school—
a special day even though it occurs once every year. Be sure to
write . . .

- what grade your child is in
- the names of teachers
- what expectations you talked about over breakfast or the
  night before
- what new supplies were used, such as a new box of crayons
  or a first set of pencils
- what surprises the day brought

Maybe even add a bit on what you remember about your own
first day of school.

Homeschoolers can write about what children learned on the
first day of the school year or some of the best questions asked

It's All in a Name

When Scott came home from his first day of
kindergarten, he told me his teacher had a helper
and her name was Mrs. Eagle.
"Are you sure that's her name?" I asked.
"Yes," he answered as he flapped his arms like
a bird.
When I went to school the next day, I met
Scott's teacher and her helper, whose name was
Mrs. Heagle.

that day. Homeschoolers can also incorporate journaling into the curriculum. Assign journal keeping to your children for a day, a week, or a course.

Birthdays—Celebrations to Remember

Your children will appreciate remembering all the details of each birthday—good and bad—because these memories help prepare them for all the future birthdays. The sky's the limit on the details you can record, but start with these:

- How and where did they celebrate?
- Was there a party with friends, or did you do something with just the family?
- What traditions were begun or replayed?
- Did they bring a birthday treat to school or to church?
- What gifts were received or party favors given?
- Was there cake or a special treat—what kind and why?
- What was planned, was a surprise, or happened unexpectedly?
- What was the best (or worst or at least memorable) thing that happened?

Of course, some birthday moments you may not want to remember, like the time Scott had the stomach flu on his seventh birthday and started throwing up as he was opening his presents. I thought I turned off the video camera, but it was still on.

He will always remember his seventh birthday the way it really happened.

Victories—You Did It!

Young children often learn and acquire skills that take time and repeated effort. Remember to record special accomplishments, such as the first time your child . . .

- holds a spoon and feeds himself
- learns to crawl
- stands up
- walks on her own
- utters first words
- says a prayer
- draws a picture
- learns to write his name
- dresses herself
- graduates from a tricycle and learns to ride a bicycle
- helps clean his room, clear the table, or do a household task

For example, Rob earned his very first blue ribbon by standing on his head the longest in his gymnastics class. When he came home, he put the ribbon in his special drawer. We still have the blue ribbon.

If you have a child with physical limitations or learning disabilities, be sure to write about any accomplishment, no matter how small it may seem. Keeping an account of his or her progress will be an encouragement to you as well.

Remember All the Boo-Boos

A child's life is full of bumps and bruises. One of your kids (or all of them!) may end up in the emergency room with a broken bone, the need for stitches, or a bean up his or her nose. This is usually a very emotional time for both mother and child. Once the trauma is over and the healing begins, write about the incident in your child's journal. Ask your child for some input to capture a fuller perspective.

Tooth-Fairy Stories

Losing baby teeth is a monumental event in the lives of all children—a sign of growing up. While some children are frightened by losing a part of their bodies, others are oblivious to the blood

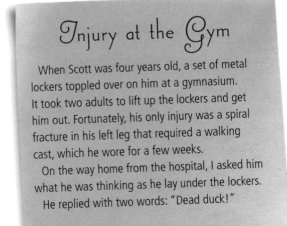

Injury at the Gym

When Scott was four years old, a set of metal lockers toppled over on him at a gymnasium. It took two adults to lift up the lockers and get him out. Fortunately, his only injury was a spiral fracture in his left leg that required a walking cast, which he wore for a few weeks.

On the way home from the hospital, I asked him what he was thinking as he lay under the lockers. He replied with two words: "Dead duck!"

and pain, because they know something magical is about to occur once they place a lost tooth under their pillow. In any case, most children have at least one memorable tooth story for a great journal entry.

For example, one time Rob had a loose tooth and was tired of having it dangle in his mouth. He asked my husband, Bob, to yank it out. Bob gave the tooth a quick jerk, but it slipped out of his fingers, and Rob accidentally swallowed it.

"Now the tooth fairy will never find it!" our son cried.

Somehow the tooth fairy knew what happened and put a surprise under Rob's pillow anyway.

In a poetry book I published several years ago, I included the following poem, which captures that loose-tooth experience. You can copy down this poem in your child's journal along with his or her own memory or—better yet—try writing your own poem together.

While Dad Was Away

Karen's husband was attending a pastor's conference in Nebraska, when out came her daughter's front tooth.

Karen saw the tooth on her daughter's nightstand that evening. She asked, "Why didn't you put your tooth under your pillow?"

"Because," her daughter replied, "the tooth fairy is in Omaha."

A Mor

Loose Tooth

My tooth came loose the other day,
It happened while I was at play.
I wiggled it with all my might,
Back and forth,
Left and right.

I twisted it around and 'round,
I pushed it up,
I pulled it down.
I couldn't take it anymore,
And so I tied it
To the door.

SLAM! BANG! Out it came.
A little blood,
A little pain.
And now I have a little hole;
It's where my tongue
Just seems to go.[1]

Because Moving Matters

In today's transient society, it's common for families to move to another neighborhood, town, and state, or even another country. Along with packing boxes comes the task of sifting through a mixed bag of emotions: excitement and anticipation for what lies ahead, fear of the unknown, and sadness for what's left behind—the closing of one chapter of your life.

Does anyone remember anything when there's so much change swirling around?

Children will recall general things about a move, if they're old enough at the time, but they'll remember the details only if you write them down.

And yet who has time to journal while in the process of moving?

Here's something you can do: jot notes next to your listed to-dos. Don't even try to write out all you want to remember—just jot down key words. Then, once you're settled in your new place, give yourself a time-out from the unpacking to write out your moving experience in greater detail.

I did this when my kids were ten, seven, and three. Our family had moved across town to a house in a more convenient location—closer to our church, Bob's office, and the athletic club we'd recently joined in an effort to stay physically fit through the long Michigan winters.

We were excited about all these things but knew we were leaving a great neighborhood with wonderful families. We felt such sadness saying good-bye to the life we'd known for nine years. The move was especially hard for Rob, since his best friend, Adam, lived three doors down.

So when moving day came, the day after Thanksgiving, we invited Adam to spend the first weekend in our new home, making the transition a little easier for Rob.

Though our home was new to us as a family, the house itself was forty years old and in need of some serious remodeling. We quickly began knocking down walls and redoing every room in the house. This required setting up a temporary kitchen in the basement, where we cooked and ate meals for the next six months, and converting the dining room to a dormitory-style bedroom with three twin beds. Our kids had a blast sleeping in the dining room for several months until their bedrooms were finally ready for occupation.

Since we did much of the work ourselves, we let our kids help in age-appropriate ways, and our moving experience turned into many months of family adventures without having to leave home. Rob thoroughly enjoyed banging a sledgehammer against the kitchen wall, and both boys helped with some of the painting. Teri helped out by "vacuuming" the new carpet with her toy vacuum cleaner—which she still keeps, seventeen years later, in her closet.

Some of our greatest family stories come from this time, and our kids love reading about them in their journals. How much would be missed without records of these details!

You can keep a family journal in a place where everyone can jot down thoughts at any time in the home you're leaving, along the way in the car, and once you arrive at the new place.

Keep this journal in a place where it won't get packed—say, inside the pillowcase of one of your pillows. Here are some questions you might pose on pages for everyone to contribute to:

- What will I miss most about our old home?
- What was my favorite room in our old home (and why)?
- What were my first impressions of our new home?
- What's the funniest thing that happened as we were packing or moving?
- What did we do on our first day and night in our new home?
- What did our new home look like before we moved in—and one month after?

During the Teen Years

Packed into your child's adolescence are comments, events, and special moments you'll want to remember, all swirling around a variety of things: sports, music, drama, teachers, coaches, friends, dating, dreams for their independence and future (college and careers they're interested in exploring). Since teenagers' emotions are unpredictable, overdramatic, and constantly changing, it's often best to stick to the facts in the journals you keep for your children during this time.

For my own children, I especially focused on positive experiences. Many teenagers face struggles and disappointments on a regular basis. As they try to rise above their circumstances, they don't need to be reminded of their failures. I know Teri will always remember the day she was the last one cut from the varsity tennis team. I didn't need to write it down in her journal to remind her. But the following year I devoted plenty of space to writing about how her hard work and determination paid off. She not only made the varsity tennis team this time, but she won a state championship!

One more word of caution about the teen years: stay out of your teen's love life! It's fine to write about homecoming dances, proms, and special dates, but stick to the facts. You can add comments like, "You looked so pretty in your dress" or "You spent four hours getting ready!" But avoid writing things like, "I think you really like this guy" or "This could be Mr. Right." Those are thoughts for your children to express in their own journals or diaries.

when life gets messy

Since life is not all sweet and humorous, there may be times when you're faced with tragic or difficult events. Divorce, death, and serious illness can become a part of your child's life. As you write about these delicate issues, be honest and share all the facts you feel necessary.

Be careful not to let your own emotions influence your writing in the journal you keep for your child. You may be angry at a

Record the wonderful things your teens might miss because they're too fixated on other matters—things like . . .
- the outcome of their accomplishments—how others are affected or how you see others responding
- how elegant, compassionate, composed, serious, smart, passionate, fun spirited, free spirited, or humble they seemed at a specific time
- any moments you treasure when you're together for rare talks or confidences (even if it's just chatter while doing the dishes)— because it's such a crazy, busy time when you're too frequently just passing one another on the way to your individual business and activities

spouse or God, but your child might not have those same feelings. Try to write from your child's perspective and offer hope where possible.

I had this task before me when Rob was eighteen years old and his friend Ryan died in a car accident. This was the greatest loss my son had ever experienced.

I wanted to express the sorrow he was feeling, but I wanted to record other things too. Ryan was a Christian, and when several teenagers accepted Christ after his funeral, I knew that was something to remember. I wrote about that and expressed the hope of seeing Ryan in heaven. There was pain on the page, but there was also rejoicing—that Ryan's life and death were not in vain, as they brought others to Jesus.

To write about the hard, painful times in your children's lives, try the following examples as jump-starters. Then write with great honesty and love about the tough moments, with an eye on the future.

- I'm sorry you have to go through this, but with God's help we'll make it.
- Today is bad, horrible. But it is one chapter in the story of your life. Tomorrow can be different—as can be the day after that and the day after that.
- I wish this didn't have to be so painful, but I believe better days are ahead.
- Sometimes things happen that we can't understand or explain. Heartache and difficulties are a part of life. But God's love is greater than our problems, and he gives us strength to get through this. He's there for us.
- John 16:33: "[Jesus said,] I have told you these things, so that you may have peace. In this world you will have trouble. But take heart! I have overcome the world!"

adopted children

Journaling for adopted children is especially meaningful. It gives these precious children a sense of roots and belonging to a family. Include any information you have about your children that they would enjoy knowing: where they were born, all the details of how much they weighed and measured and what color hair and eyes they had, perhaps even (if and when the time is right) what

Start a family (not stepfamily) journal that unites all of you from the moment you begin blending. Let this represent a new beginning. Remind one another that every day is like a new page: clean, fresh, waiting for memories to be made, filled with possibility. Take turns writing in the journal, noting the date and the name of the person making the entry. You can leave the journal in an easily accessible place where everyone can jot down something special at any time, or perhaps you can take turns being the journal keeper.

you know about their birth parents—details every person longs to know about his or her roots.

Write about the adoption process and how eager you were to have your child become part of the family. Share some of the prayers you prayed when you asked God to bless you with children. Describe in detail the events that occurred on the day your child came to live with you. Remind your chosen child over and over again how happy you are that God picked him or her to be in your family.

Journal for your adopted child. Simply promise yourself to randomly jot down what's in your heart for your chosen child. Date your entries so your heart messages will show a lifetime of love—a beginning, a middle, and no end.

- Are you smiling at the way your daughter tried dressing up the dog in doll clothes today? Write about that little moment.

- Did your son make you laugh at how quick he is to play in the mud while you garden? Write about that.

- When your teenagers get moody and want some space from you, write about your feelings—how much you want to hold them close but how proud you are to see them grow into young adults.

the blended family

If stepchildren are added to your family, begin journaling for them as you would for your own children, especially if they are young. Doing so can bring a sense of unity to your new family unit.

Focus on the positive times you share and the special moments you want stepchildren to remember. It's possible that they may not be interested in the journals you write for them; it's also possible that they'll be forever grateful—you cared enough for them at the moment and beyond to record positive things.

remember the grandparents

In the natural progression of life, most children will experience the death of a grandparent or great-grandparent. To help preserve the memory of these loved ones and ancestors, create a photo journal or scrapbook of your children's grandparents and great-grandparents.

Collect pictures of fun family times, and include a sentence or two about each picture. Include any cards or letters received from grandparents. Involve Grandma or Grandpa when they come to visit. Ask them to jot down their memories about photos of them or letters they wrote or about memories in the making.

Talk about the Good Ol' Days

Keep a journal of interviews with your children's grandparents. Ask them about their favorite summer or winter activities, what their favorite color is, and how things were in the days when they were growing up.

- How did they get around?
- What kind of phone was in their house?
- Did they write letters, type them, send email, or use faxes?
- Did they have a favorite saying or remember a saying their fathers and mothers often repeated?
- What did they do for fun or in their spare time?
- What was their favorite year (or what are their favorite seasons) and why?
- Other favorites are great to record: favorite meal, book, music, film, TV show, Bible book or passage, tree or flower, car, place, or pet.

For more ideas on interview questions, contact the National Grandparents Day Council, a nonprofit corporation established by descendants of Marian H. McQuade, the founder of National Grandparents Day. Send a self-addressed, stamped envelope and a request for "Grandparent Interview Questions" to 1449 Antero Drive, Loveland, CO 80538 or visit the council's website at http://www. grandparents-day.com/interview.htm.

If any of the grandparents have already passed away, it's not too late. Search through boxes or drawers for cards, letters, pictures, or anything you might have that can be put into an album.

A scrapbook, photo album, or journal of grandparents will remind your children of the special love that was shared and the events that were celebrated.

feeling creative?

Write poetry for your children. You can do this, being serious or silly, in short bits or in long passages. However you fashion your poems, be sure to feature your child's unique characteristics or express your own thoughts and feelings.

Use any of the following poems to inspire your own or copy them into your journals for your children as "starter" pages.

Remember: Your children will love the poems you write for them. The results need not seem professional or like fine literature, just loving and personal—whatever comes to your mind and from your heart.

The Acrostic Poem

This form is very simple! Write your child's name vertically and use descriptive words that begin with each letter. See the two examples below, which use the names Andrew and Beth. To elaborate, below each acrostic poem you can get more detailed: "*A* is for adorable, because that describes your smile. *N* is for nutty, because you like to do handstands all over the house. *D* is for delightful, because . . ."

Adorable
Nutty
Delightful
Rambunctious
Energetic
Wonderful

Beautiful
Enthusiastic
Thoughtful
Happy

The Rhyming Poem

This form of poetry can be as playful to write as to read. Try this simple exercise first: begin lines with, or feature prominently, the words *your* or *you*. Or try forming a whole poem like "Favorite Things, on page 38," by rhyming just the words *you* and *too*.

You

Your hair is red.
Your eyes are brown.
You love to jump and run around.
You don't like broccoli, beans, or peas.
You kindly say, "No thank you, please."
But you're my very precious child,
Sometimes gentle and sometimes wild.
And so I thank the Lord above
For giving you to me to love.

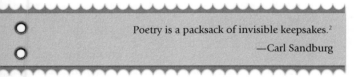

Poetry is a packsack of invisible keepsakes.[2]
—Carl Sandburg

I Love You

I love your eyes, I love your nose,

And all of you, from head to toes.

I love your sweet and tender ways,

Your laughter brightens all my days.

I love your hugs, I love your smile.

I love it when we talk awhile.

I love to watch you when you play,

I love you more and more each day.

One of a Kind

There's nobody like you, you're one of a kind.

No one but you has your heart, soul, or mind.

For you were designed by your Father above,

Made in his image because of his love.

He fashioned and formed you to be as you are,

Just as he made every twinkling star.

He gave you your voice and your very own style.

Your face is unique with your own special smile.

God made you and loves you; he knows you by name.

And though he's made millions, no two are the same.

You're wonderful, priceless, fantastic, and fine.

There's nobody like you—

You're one of a kind!

$\mathcal{P}$oetry $\mathfrak{f}$rom $\mathcal{E}$veryday $\mathcal{L}$ife

Some of the most beautiful poems aren't poetry at all—they're song lyrics or lines from a novel, chants at the high school football game, kids' blurts on the playground, recipes, notes of thanks, prayers, psalms of thanksgiving, laments, or heart cries heard on the news. Collect the lines and phrases you love and that speak to you and your children about your lives. Copy them into the journals you keep for your children. Now put them in a context: in a paragraph, write out why each snippet seemed important. Tell how it caught your attention.

Favorite Things

You like trucks and dinosaurs.

You like ice cream too.

You like castles in the sand,

But I like you.

You like ducks and fuzzy bears.

You like puppies too.

You like bedtime storybooks,

But I like you.

You like playing hide-and-seek.

You like popcorn too.

You like singing happy songs,

But I like you.

The Prose Poem

Poems that don't rhyme may be easier for you to write—and they can be more flowing, from the heart. Try writing your own prose poem, or copy the following into your kid's journal.

I Thought about You Today

I thought about you today.
I pictured you at school raising your hand,
    because you know lots of answers.
I thought about you at lunch time
    sharing your cookie with someone who didn't have one,
    because you are so kind.
I thought about you at recess
    playing with someone who was playing alone,
    because you are a good friend.
I thought about you on the bus,
    knowing you said thank you to the bus driver,
    because you are polite.
I thought about you running through the door
    and putting your arms around me
    and giving me a great big hug,
    because that is the best part of my day.
I thought about you today,
    because I love you very much.

> I like nonsense. It wakes up the brain cells. Fantasy is a necessary ingredient in living. It's a way of looking at life through the wrong end of a telescope, which is what I do, and that enables you to laugh at life's realities.[3]
>
> —Theodor Geisel, a.k.a. Dr. Seuss

poetry even non-poets can write

If you love and appreciate poetry but just don't want to try your own hand at it, you can still add poems into journals for your kids. Copy down the poems you love and who they're by, where you read each poem and when, and why each seemed important to you and meaningful for your child. You can clip things from your newspapers and magazines and tape them in your journals as well. Be sure to note the dates. Years and generations later, your children will treasure these pages that powerfully speak to them in the words of a poet.

experience it!

You don't have to wait for something exciting or unexpected to happen before you have good stories for your kids' journals. Create experiences by planning or spontaneously engaging in fun activities.

Walk on the Wild Side

Take a nature walk with your child and be sure to bring along a notebook, pencil, and paper bag. As you walk write down the sights you see, sounds you hear, and aromas you smell. Collect treasures in your bag along the way: shells, rocks and stones, leaves, funny-shaped twigs, nuts, pinecones. When you return home, write a story with your child about the adventure and make a collage with the treasures you picked up along the way.

Indoor Camping

When the winter blahs make your kids restless, go on a camping adventure—indoors. Pull out the sleeping bags, and let your kids sleep on the floor in the family room or playroom. Make popcorn, tell stories, sing songs around a pretend campfire (or use your fireplace). Your kids' imaginations will soar as they enjoy their indoor camping trip. Whatever you do, pretend you're in the great outdoors, meaning no TV or videos allowed!

Family Picnic

Original? Of course not! But many families get so busy that they overlook this easy and fun activity. The trick is to keep it simple. All you need are a few basic items: sandwiches or hot dogs, a bag of chips, pieces of fruit, bottled water or a jug of lemonade, and a bag of cookies. Throw in some napkins, paper plates, a blanket or beach towel, and a Frisbee, and you're ready to go. Where? If you have a park nearby, that's fine. Otherwise, the backyard will work just as well. When you return home, pull out the journals or jot a note on the calendar so your kids will always remember your fun family activities.

add Bible verses

Remind your children of God's love and care by writing Bible verses that are especially meaningful to you or to them in their journals. For a simpler text, use a children's translation if you have one. There are numerous possibilities, but here are a few examples of great verses to comfort and encourage your children through life:

- **Joshua 1:9**—"Do not be afraid or discouraged. For the LORD your God is with you wherever you go" (NLT).
- **Psalm 118:1**—"Give thanks to the LORD, because he is good. His faithful love continues forever" (NIrV).
- **Psalm 121:8**—"The LORD keeps watch over you as you come and go, both now and forever" (NLT).
- **Proverbs 16:9**—"In your heart you plan your life. But the LORD decides where your steps will take you" (NIrV). (A great graduation verse!)
- **Philippians 1:6**—"God began doing a good work in you. And he will continue it until it is finished when Jesus Christ comes again. I am sure of that" (ICB).
- **1 Peter 5:7**—"Give all your worries to him, because he cares for you" (ICB).

share the journals

For many years I didn't tell my children I was writing journals for them. I wanted to go about journaling in secret and someday, on a milestone, meaningful occasion, surprise them by giving them their childhood memories in a book.

Then, one day as I sat at the kitchen counter and entered a few new excerpts in each of their journals, I turned back the pages and read some of the things recorded over the years. I laughed and cried and decided this was too good to keep to myself.

That night at the dinner table, toward the end of our meal, I brought out the journals. "We are going to do something a little different for our family devotions," I announced. As I shared a few excerpts from each of their journals, the kids howled with laughter and begged for more. We stayed around the dinner table for more than an hour, enjoying the stories that brought back many great memories. That in itself became a memory for each of their books!

Then, once my kids knew I was writing journals for them, they often told me about things I might not have known otherwise so I could make note of it in their memory books. Often, if we were together when something interesting or humorous occurred, we'd look at each other, and they would say, "Be sure to write that in my journal, Mom!"

The journals became a special bond for us. They also came in handy when English teachers gave my kids assignments that required writing about a childhood experience. There on my desk were books just about them filled with plenty of ideas.

I know it would have been fun to have saved the journals as some future surprise for my children, but I'm glad I decided to share these keepsakes with them while they were growing up. We're sharing the joy—and the treasure—together.

it's never too late!

If your kids are grown or almost grown, don't just wish you'd kept journals for them—start preserving memories now from what you remember. You may surprise yourself and, as you start recording a few things, find that you recall more.

Protect yourself from feeling overwhelmed, especially if you have several children and want to create journals for each one. Focus on each child separately, one at a time. Don't be surprised, however, if some of the memories involve more than one child. This can help you record the same story in the sibling's journal and help you make more progress than you imagined.

The following suggestions will help identify even more key seasons of life where there are memories waiting to be harvested.

Birth

Do you remember when and where your child was born? Okay, that's where you start! Since giving birth is a rather significant experience, you should be able to recall a few details about the place, the time, who was there, what happened around you, what was in the news on the day your child was born—that sort of thing. Write down everything you can remember about the events surrounding your child's birth.

Now add pages about early childhood events:

- Do you remember when your child took his first step or said her first word?

- What was his favorite food, toy, or stuffed animal?

- Who were your child's babysitters?

- Describe your child's nursery or a favorite blanket.

Do these busy years seem a blank? In an encyclopedia or online, look up important events during these years. Events can trigger memories of where you were and what you were doing.

If you run out of words and have a few baby pictures, paste them into the journal. Pictures alone help tell the story.

Cut yourself some slack as you create. It doesn't matter if you don't remember the exact dates that things occurred. Just write whatever you do remember—or ask others who were there what they remember. You will be giving your child something only you can—remembrances of roots.

Preschool Years

Remember these years, when your child's personality began to blossom? Write down whatever you recall. Look through photo albums or shoe boxes filled with old snapshots. Photographs are good memory joggers, and most pictures have a story behind them that only you can tell. Jog your memories with the following questions, and don't worry about writing a journal story so much as just noting random memories as they come:

- What were your child's favorite storybooks, games, or songs?

- Did she have a special outfit she wore to church or a pair of pajamas that *had* to be worn every night? (My boys each had a pair of cowboy boots they never wanted to take off!)
- Who were your child's friends? Did he play with neighbors, preschool friends, or cousins?
- Did your child move out of her nursery to another bedroom in the house?
- Where did you live during these years? Describe what your house looked like.
- Did you have any pets?

Elementary School Years

These were busy years when your child probably seemed to change every time you turned around. Write whatever details you can remember—and don't forget about the holidays, birthdays, and summer vacations.

- Where did your child go to elementary school?
- Did he travel by bus, carpool, bicycle, or legs (his or yours)?
- Who were your child's favorite teachers and classmates?
- What was your child's favorite subject?
- What did your child do when she came home from school?
- Where did you live?
- What was your child's room like?
- What favorite foods or snacks were always requested?

Middle School Years

These are the years when most kids begin to get involved in sports, band, choir, and other extracurricular activities. Just like in elementary school, your child may have had special teachers and friends you can mention. But these years should also provide you with many after-school, weekend, and summer activities to write about.

- What passions did your child begin to show in hobbies, interests, and activities?
- What signs of a budding adult began to show?
- In what ways was your child still innocent and childlike in these years?
- Who were your child's friends, classmates, or teammates?
- Where did you live?
- Did your child go to any sports camps or summer camps?
- Did your family take any vacations during these years?
- What special accomplishments did your child experience?

High School Years

This is when your child began to really seek independence and you learned to let go in a million little ways, or big ones if you were forced to do so. As you record memories and any details, express how proud you are of your child's accomplishments, character, and personality. Let your child hear now how much you love and believe in him or her.

- Where did your child go to high school?
- What activities was he involved in?

- Did she participate in any special programs or plays?
- Did he have a summer job?
- Who were her friends?
- Was he involved in a youth group at church or go on any mission trips?
- What trips or vacations did you take as a family during her high school years?
- What colleges did he visit and apply to?
- How did your family celebrate her graduation from high school?
- What college or career choices did he make?

the worth of jotted memories

Once you start writing about your children's lives, you may be surprised at how much you remember, how easy the practice is, and what fun you're having in the process.

As the variety of ideas here show, journals can be as creative and individual as fingerprints. No two need resemble one another. And journals can feed on so many things—not just your memories but those of your children's grandparents, siblings, and close friends.

As each journal fills up, think about a special time to give these "all about you" books to your children. However your journals turn out, celebrate the fact that each one is a one-of-a-kind treasure, something no one else could create, a priceless gift filled with the wonders of heaven and earth, because between the pages are memories and dreams—and heart.

Write a Birthday Letter—Write a letter to your child on his or her birthday every year. Include highlights of the past year and notes about his or her interests and activities during the year. If you keep these birthday letters in a personal folder or binder, they'll begin to accumulate. In just a few years, you'll have already amassed wonderful memories to share without the demands of frequent journaling. You can even make a tradition each year of rereading the letters from years past.

Save Those Merry Christmas Letters—If you send Christmas letters to friends and relatives each year, save them! Christmas letters are usually a brief summary of the past twelve months and in time can hold treasured memories over the decades.

Create a Family Album—One journal for the whole family can be an especially convenient and manageable treasure for folks with lots of kids or little time (or both!). You can still recognize individuals in a family journal: highlight one child at a time on special days such as birthdays or graduations. Be sure, when keeping this kind of journal, to pick a booklet that can be easily reproduced, as your children are likely to want their own copies someday.

Keep Individual Calendars—Buy a calendar for each of your children every year and give it to him or her for Christmas. Keep the calendars in a convenient place, and use them as you would a journal. The great thing about this approach: the entry dates are already provided—and usually there are just nuggets of space for short notes, not long entries.

Go Electronic—If you use the computer on a regular basis, create files for each of your children and save e-notes for them. Some moms really like the convenience and speed of revising journal entries this way, but be sure to store your entries on a disc, CD, or hardcopy in the event your trusty computer has a major meltdown. The other alternative is to record memories—literally. Make audio- or videotapes (or both) of special moments with the kids. One afternoon when my kids were young, I turned on the tape recorder as we read our favorite books together. The precious sound of their toddler voices mispronouncing the words is now frozen in time—a wonder for all of us.

Get Wired—When Rob went away to college, we received emails from him almost daily. Some were lengthy and detailed, while others were very short. (One message was only two words: "I'm sick!") We printed and saved his emails so he would have a journal of his first year at college.

2

celebrate throughout the year

Holiday Journals, Traditions,
and Family Rituals

Holiday Journals

Holidays are always worth remembering as a family, since that's often how they're celebrated—together. Maybe your celebrations are numerous, major events that involve travel to visit relatives or to convene at a special place. Or maybe you celebrate just a few times a year with simple pleasures centered around an elegant feast and honored traditions. In any case, the great thing about preserving the memories from such times is that you have to collect your thoughts and keepsakes into a book for each celebration only once a year!

For holidays such as Valentine's Day, Easter, Memorial Day, or the Fourth of July, I write a brief entry in each of my kids' journals, highlighting the special events of the day. But for Thanksgiving and Christmas, I use additional holiday journals to collect memories of our major family celebrations.

Thanksgiving

One year Bob and I decided not to attend our church's Thanksgiving service because our young boys both had colds. I felt badly too, as I couldn't remember a time when I hadn't attended a Thanksgiving service.

Then I had an idea: we could have our own Thanksgiving service right in our living room. So we did. We read Psalm 150, sang a couple of praise songs, offered a prayer of Thanksgiving, and counted our blessings.

It was a precious experience that I wanted to remember, so I wrote about it in a blank journal I happened to have in my desk drawer. That was the first entry in what became our Thanksgiving journal.

I quickly realized how easy and manageable it is to keep a Thanksgiving journal. Now I've been making an annual Thanksgiving entry for more than two decades and can read pages and pages of fond memories that have accumulated. A common theme involves our tradition each year of sharing gratitude for specific things as we gather around the table for Thanksgiving dinner.

Our journal tells the story: some years we were thankful for a new friend, family member, or new president; other years we were thankful for spiritual blessings, safety and health, and loving

> Include a psalm of praise, such as Psalm 100, Psalm 105:1–4, Psalm 136, or Psalm 147:1–11, in your Thanksgiving journal. Now try writing a psalm of your own as a family.

grandparents. In addition to recording specific blessings, I also include how we spend the day, and even the entire weekend. As our children grew, so did our Thanksgiving weekend activities. From football games and tennis tournaments to Christmas shopping and decorating, our Thanksgiving weekends have been busy, fun, and full of memories. But the main focus of our Thanksgiving journal is an acknowledgment of what God has done and is doing in each of our lives. It is a testament to God's provision and goodness to always be with us. It is our memorial stone.

Christmas

As we celebrate the birth of our Savior each year, we also celebrate the love we have for our family and friends—sentiments well preserved and cherished in a family Christmas journal. Just like our Thanksgiving journal, the Christmas journal requires only an annual entry.

I purchased our Christmas journal from a mail-order catalog—the only time I ever splurged on a keepsake book. This one is extra special because it features our last name, beautifully engraved, on the cover. It also allows, every year, a two-page spread with plenty of room for recording events and pasting pictures.

Each Christmas I jot down the important details of our parties, including where and with whom we celebrated. Then I include a sample of the Christmas card we sent, plus a picture or two. This memory keeper is as much fun to add to as it is to read.

Here are three different ways you can create your own Christmas journal. Maybe one will be right for you:

- For an easy but elegant-looking Christmas journal, purchase a red scrapbook from a craft or office supply store. Use permanent marker or a gold pen to write your family's name on the front.

- Glue a sheet of red felt to the front of an ordinary notebook. Decorate the cover with cutouts or shapes from various pieces of felt, using contrasting colors (example: green Christmas tree, yellow star, or white angel). You can trace around cookie cutters for the cutout shapes or buy Christmas stencils at a craft store. Cut out a rectangle and create a decorative edge with pinking shears. Write your

A Special Visitor

Though all of the pictures in our Christmas journal have a special meaning, the picture from our 1984 Christmas is probably my favorite. That's the year—on December 8—our only girl, Teri, was born. And someone else showed up on our doorstep too . . .

We lived in a neighborhood with many young families and seemingly tons of kids, plus a retired couple who thoroughly enjoyed the antics of all the kiddos. Every year this couple would dress up as Mr. and Mrs. Santa Claus and go door-to-door visiting every family. (Imagine! I never had to stand in long lines at the mall for pictures of the kids with Santa, and since we never knew exactly what night Santa and his missus would be coming, every day in December my children were extra good!) So in our Christmas journal, for 1984 I have an extra-special picture of that year's most treasured gift—six-day-old Teri in the arms of Santa and Mrs. Claus, who sat in our living room.

family's name on the rectangle and glue it to the front of the notebook.

- Buy a package of letter-size Christmas stationery and use it to record your Christmas events and memories. You can write with a colorful pen (red or green) or use the computer if you prefer. Save the pages in a folder or binder, and in a few years, they will become holiday treasures.

family traditions

The traditions you honor are simply repeated activities especially dear or unique to your family. Children especially enjoy traditions for the sense of security, belonging, and purpose created by repeated rituals or events. Traditions seem to say to them, "We have a special family, and this is what our family does."

The holidays are a great time to establish or continue family traditions, but traditions can also be honored throughout the entire year. The following ideas and suggestions (all journal worthy!) are easy-to-implement traditions that may fit your family and give

These visits from Mr. and Mrs. Claus added extra excitement to other Christmases too. One year when we were Christmas shopping, Rob saw a figurine of Santa bowing at the manger of baby Jesus. He grabbed it from the shelf, exclaiming, "We have to buy this and give it to Mr. and Mrs. Santa."

So we did, and a few days after their visit, we received another blessing—a note that read, "Dear Bowman family, thank you for the beautiful figurine. We too believe in the real meaning of Christmas. Love, Mr. and Mrs. Santa Claus."

you something to write about and remember for years to come. Please keep in mind this is not a to-do list! Pick and choose what appeals to you and your family's interests.

Ideas for Thanksgiving Traditions

Share Bible Verses

Put a note card with a Bible verse of praise or thanksgiving (you can find lots of them in the book of Psalms) on each plate at the dinner table. Have each person read his or her verse before you eat your Thanksgiving meal.

Thanksgiving Prayer

Hold hands around the dinner table, and offer a sentence prayer in which each person says thank you to God for something specific:

"Thank you, God, for our home."

"Thank you, God, for our pastor."

"Thank you, God, for Grandma and Grandpa."

"Thank you, God, for pumpkin pie."

Corn Kernels

Give every person a kernel of corn, then begin to pass an empty basket from one person to the next at the table. As each person hands the basket to the next, have him or her deposit the corn kernel and share what he or she is thankful for. Keep the basket on the table for a few days so that the corn kernels are a reminder of your blessings.

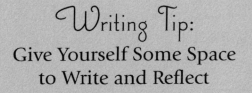

Writing Tip:
Give Yourself Some Space to Write and Reflect

Do you have a special place that inspires you to reminisce, relax, and recall or record memories? Create one. Maybe you don't have a room of your own or a desk. No matter. What about the kitchen table after the family's out of the house or a chair in the corner of the living room? Keep memory-catcher tools in a basket by your side: pens, paper, notebooks, tape, glue, scissors, and perhaps a Polaroid or disposable camera. Maybe you prefer the silence on the porch in a rickety porch swing or just down the road at a table in a favorite coffee shop.

Maybe the "place" you need isn't so much physical as emotional and with the right ambiance. Create the right mood with scented candles or fresh air from an open window, with music from the stereo or your pet by your side.

Share the Thanksgiving Story

Go to your local library or bookstore and find a children's picture book on the story of Thanksgiving that you can read to your children.

Here are a few recommendations:

- *Thanksgiving: A Time to Remember*, by Barbara Rainey (Crossway Books, 2002). The story, which includes historical facts and solid Christian content, is meant to be read aloud by families on Thanksgiving Day. It also includes a CD of Thanksgiving music for the whole family to enjoy.

- *Squanto and the Miracle of Thanksgiving,* by Eric Metaxas (Tommy Nelson, 1999). This book focuses on the religious roots of Thanksgiving and features the life of Squanto, who suffered many hardships and eventually became a friend and helper of the Pilgrims.

- *A Pioneer Thanksgiving: A Story of Harvest Celebrations in 1841,* by Barbara Greenwood (Kids Can Press, 1999). Factual information about American pioneers is presented through a fictional story. Includes recipes, craft projects, and games.

- *The Story of Thanksgiving,* by Nancy J. Skarmeas (Ideals Publications, 1999). This board book for preschoolers tells about the first Thanksgiving in a short and simple format.

Ideas for Christmas Traditions

Getaways

When our children were in elementary school, we felt that the busyness of the holiday season often robbed us of quality family time. We decided to start a family tradition of having a pre-Christmas weekend getaway. It meant being organized and getting the shopping done early, but it was well worth the effort. For several years, on the weekend before Christmas, we headed north for some great winter skiing. It proved to be perfect timing: preseason ski prices were low, the lift lines were short, and the slopes were wide open. Our weekend ski trip not only became a favorite

A Mom's Guide to Making Memories Last

family tradition but also provided us with hours of family fun and great memories.

You can plan a pre-Christmas getaway as well. Your trip need not be an overnight one or anything costly, just something you can enjoy doing together. Many of these ideas are free at local churches or cost little in most communities:

- Attend a live nativity.
- Take in a Christmas play or even a ballet.
- Listen to a musical performance, whether it's a Christmas pops concert at the symphony, Handel's *Messiah* sung by a choir, or a family sing-along around the community tree.
- If you're an outdoor adventure family, schedule a Friday night or Saturday to go biking, sledding, or ice skating.
- Take an evening drive to see Christmas lights, even if they're just the stars in the sky.

Advent Calendars

Advent calendars are a great idea for young children, especially since the days between Thanksgiving and Christmas seem like an eternity. An advent calendar allows you to celebrate each day and enjoy the anticipation of an approaching holiday.

Some years I purchased advent calendars with little flaps to open, revealing a holiday picture. Other years I simply made my own December calendar out of green construction paper and taped it on the refrigerator. Then the kids took turns putting a Christmas sticker on the calendar on each new day.

The homemade calendar is just as much fun as the store-bought calendar, and the idea can be adapted for any special event you anticipate.

Christmas at the Table

Buy an inexpensive set of Christmas dishes to use with your children throughout the month of December. Every time you sit down to eat with your family, the dishes will remind them of the special holiday that will soon be here. It will add to the excitement and anticipation of this joyous event. The dishes may also become a family keepsake to pass down to the next generation.

Putting Up the Christmas Tree

When I was growing up, my dad was in charge of putting up the Christmas tree every year, and the rest of us were eager to help. As my mother brought out heaps of ornaments and tree trimmings, my sisters, brother, and I would dig through the boxes to find our favorite decorations.

Our order for decorating never differed: first the lights went on the tree, then the ornaments, then garland and silver icicles.

Surprise Guests

Through the years we've established some Christmas traditions that we try to repeat each holiday season, but we've also had some unique once-in-a-lifetime experiences. One year we traveled to California for Christmas with an aunt, uncle, and cousins whom we rarely get to see—and our California aunt has some traditions that must be honored, regardless of who's visiting.

One of those traditions is to dress formally for Christmas Eve dinner. Her teenage granddaughters put a new twist on the evening by dressing in sport coats and ties, and my nine- and twelve-year-old boys got into the spirit too. They came to dinner wearing dresses and wigs!

Everyone loved the surprise, and it certainly added some flavor to our Christmas Eve dinner and another great picture for the Christmas journal.

When the tree was finally decorated and the lights were plugged in, I sat in the glow and waited and watched.

Some of the lights had liquid inside that bubbled when the liquid got warm. With those first bubbles, I knew Christmas season had officially arrived.

How do you mark the beginning of the season? Play Christmas music? Decorate the halls? If you do set up a Christmas tree . . .

- plan to decorate it together, as a family event
- choose a good time when everyone can participate
- set the mood with scented candles and background music or carols you sing
- let your kids help in any way they can; it's probably easier for you to decorate yourself, but your children will enjoy hanging the ornaments and garland
- play a game together afterward or read a Christmas story
- have two Christmas trees—one for you and one for the kids. We have a formal, elegant tree in our living room, with gold trimmings, glass ornaments, and artificial roses. In the family room, we have our "family" tree with all the sentimental ornaments collected through the years, from teddy bears and reindeer to nutcrackers and baby Jesus.

Classic Christmas Reads

One of my favorite books is *The Christmas Miracle of Jonathan Toomey*, by Susan Wojciehowski (Candlewick Press, 1995). The lengthy text is not designed for little ones, but older children will enjoy this story of how a young boy's insight into a wooden nativity set melted the heart of a grieving woodcarver.

And remember, moms—even though your kids may be good readers, they still enjoy having you read a good story to them.

For the little ones: I have recently written two board books for preschoolers: *J Is for Jesus* and *Jesus, Me, and My Christmas Tree* (ZonderKidz, 2005). Little ones will love the size and shape of these sturdy books, and moms will enjoy sharing the true meaning of Christmas with their children.

The Nativity

Display a nativity set in a prominent place in your home so that everyone can see it. Next to the nativity, place a Bible opened to the Christmas story found in the second chapter of Luke—a bold statement regarding your beliefs and a way of enticing you again and again to focus on the real story of Christmas.

Some families wait until Christmas Eve to add baby Jesus to the display as a way of helping young children understand that many people eagerly awaited the Savior's birth.

Ask yourself, *How might I use my nativity set every day to visually, tactilely remind me of the anticipation felt and the distance crossed to find Jesus—and for him to come to us?* This could be something you answer—and journal about—anew every year.

Christmas Cards

The Christmas cards, pictures, and letters you receive each year from friends and relatives are not just for you—they're for your whole family.

- Share them at the dinner table every evening during the Christmas season.

- Pray together over each one—say a prayer of gratitude that the senders are in your lives and pray for their needs.
- Keep the letters in a notebook or basket where they can be reread throughout the Christmas season—or save the special letters in a notebook for keeps.

A Birthday Party for Jesus

To help your children appreciate the true meaning of Christmas, make a birthday cake and sing "Happy Birthday" to Jesus. You can celebrate Jesus's birthday with your own family or use this idea as an evangelical outreach in your neighborhood. Make it even more special these ways:

- Send out invitations.
- Ask everyone to bring a small gift to donate to a local charity.
- Before you cut the birthday cake, read the Christmas story from the Bible or from a children's book that gives the biblical account.

Choose a Charity

How, in a society caught up in the anticipation of receiving gifts, can you reinforce the importance of giving?

Our church provides empty shoe boxes for families to take home and fill with items for needy children. After the shoe boxes are filled with hygiene products, treats, and toys, they're returned with the proper amount of postage and sent as Christmas gifts to children in other countries.

My kids loved picking out items to place in their shoe boxes each year; the tradition has taught them the joy of giving, especially to those in need.

One year as I was putting the final items in our family shoe box, Teri came to me with a letter she'd written. "This needs to go in the box too," she said, handing me the carefully folded paper. "It's how the real meaning of Christmas is about baby Jesus and how he was born so he could save us from our sins. It's about how to ask Jesus into our hearts." Teri's letter became the most important item in the shoe box that year.

Christmas Ornaments

Giving your children a Christmas ornament every year is a fun and easy tradition that can continue all their lives. My mother started this with Teri, giving her a Christmas ornament every December 8 for her birthday. Some of the ornaments are humorous, and others are simply beautiful, but every one is special.

The practical benefit of this tradition: when your kids grow up and leave home, they'll already have a collection of ornaments—and memories.

Christmas Movies

One of my favorite holiday movies is *A Charlie Brown Christmas.* When Charlie Brown becomes exasperated by all the holiday nonsense, he finally cries out in despair, "Isn't there anyone who

Make Your Own Movie— and Memory

Have your own camcorder or movie camera? Get the kids to do a reenactment of their favorite Christmas film or even act out a play they create on their own—something short and simple. Let spontaneity rule. If you give the kids something to do or pretend to be doing, they might even forget the camera's on them. Then set the lights, turn on the camcorder, get silly, and savor those holiday moments.

knows what Christmas is all about?" Of course, that's when little Linus offers him comfort by reciting the Christmas story from the Gospel of Luke. What a simple yet powerful scene that captures the attention of both children and adults while presenting the gospel message.

There are so many other good Christmas movies from which to choose. You have favorites, I'm sure. Why not make a tradition of watching one of your favorites together as a family? Attach to this time something unique for your family: sipping homemade cocoa with marshmallows, lighting a special Christmas candle, turning down the lights, and making a ceremony of flipping on the Christmas lights.

Remember the Lonely

I have a cousin who's been in a nursing home most of her adult life. She's never had a husband, children, or a home of her own. For many years she lived in a nursing home near our home, so my children and I went to visit her from time to time. She loved our visits and proudly displayed on her wall the pictures my kids drew for her.

At Christmas we always brought her a small plant or figurine to bring cheer to her nightstand, and she wouldn't let us leave until we sang some Christmas songs.

Funny thing, though, and it never failed: we'd plan a visit, intent on cheering her up, but we were the ones blessed by the time we left. My cousin's positive attitude and grateful spirit reminded us over and over how much we have to be thankful for; we were inspired by her humbleness.

Who do you know—or who can you find—who is living alone? Bring your children over for a visit or invite those who are alone to have Christmas dinner with you. The meaning and memory of such a tradition will become sweeter as the years go by.

Survive Christmas Chaos in Style

Christmas becomes unnecessarily unpleasant or chaotic when two or more sides of the family expect you to celebrate with them on the same day. Honestly, is it really worth it to spend more time on the road Christmas Day than you do at a family party? Consider these reasonable compromises:

- Christmas doesn't need to be celebrated only on December 25 to make it the real thing! Celebrate Christmas Eve with one side of the family and Christmas Day (or the day after) with the other side of the family.

A Mom's Guide to Making Memories Last

- Alternate going to one family party one year and another family party the next year.
- Celebrate Christmas week with one side of the family, then New Year's week with the other.

If you do propose a change of plans, don't expect everyone to understand your situation. In fact, some of your family members may become hurt or angry. But you and your husband need to discuss your plans and decide what is reasonable for your family and do what works best for you. Your relatives will eventually accept the new arrangements if you continue to make a sincere effort to spend quality time with them, even if it isn't on December 25.

Remind yourself that it's wonderful when a family tradition can be passed down from one generation to the next—but it's sometimes necessary to start new traditions as the family unit changes.

Moms, set a great example long before Christmas. Write thank-you notes to your children for the joy they give to you! Put a stamp on your thank-you note and mail it to the house. Young children especially will delight in receiving personal mail.

Plant the Makings for Gratitude

Start your own note-of-appreciation tradition by adding a package of thank-you cards and stamps to everyone's Christmas stockings. Or make postcards from large blank index cards that you decorate on one side with collage creations made from recycled Christmas cards, wrapping paper, and ribbon.

Say Thank You

Guess what my kids always had to do the morning after Christmas? Write thank-you notes for their Christmas presents! You can call it a discipline or a chore, but it's the right thing to do, and at our house we call it a fun tradition.

We started by giving our kids their very own stationery and return address labels; we learned that taking the time to say thank you teaches gratitude and a heightened sense of appreciation for the generosity of others. Thank-you notes also bless the people who receive them, extending the joy of Christmas long after December 25 has come and gone.

Once you begin this tradition, you'll see how writing thank-you notes is a great tradition throughout the year, and not just for gifts received but also for the ongoing contributions and personal investments of time and attention from special people like teachers and coaches.

When Troubles Mark the Holidays

The holidays provide us with hours of family togetherness, but they can also be times of stress, as many families know. Tensions can rise. Tempers can flare. Realities can collide, with conflicting expectations of how things should be.

Worse, the holidays can become downright miserable when you're facing certain sadness, such as the death of a loved one, a serious illness, a bitter divorce, or geographic separation from those you love. In any of these circumstances, holiday traditions can seem like cruel reminders that life is ever changing, losses are inevitable, and loneliness is yours.

At times like these, it helps to take the focus off yourself and focus on others instead. Starting new traditions can help you feel empowered and hopeful. Children especially can be encouraged by creating new memories or "starting over." Try out these practices that will give you something to write about as you create positive new memories:

- Have your children make Christmas cards or pictures and bring them to a nursing home.

The Very Unmerry Christmas

One Christmas Eve I was furious because my mother-in-law bought a pan of frozen lasagna after I spent all afternoon making the Italian dish she had asked me to bring. For some reason, she thought I was coming empty-handed, and I decided to make a serious issue out of the incident. I fumed all the way to her house, ranting and raving about how I'm responsible enough to bring what I'm asked to bring. When we arrived, however, my mother-in-law answered the door with tears in her eyes. A million thoughts raced through my mind as she shared the news that my husband's grandfather had just been killed in a car accident. Suddenly I was ashamed of my attitude. A pan of lasagna didn't matter. My family did.

Unfortunately, not all of our holiday celebrations are joyous occasions. As you record the events of your family gatherings, try to focus on what's important and the hopes, despite the fears, that you want to remember.

- If you have an elderly person in your neighborhood, offer to help decorate his or her home for the holidays.

- Invite a single mom to bring her kids to your house and make Christmas cookies together.

- Volunteer to work in the nursery during the Christmas Eve service if it's too difficult for you to sit through the service.

- Invite anyone who expects to be alone on Christmas Day to instead join your family celebration.

Celebrating Easter

Religious holidays offer parents the opportunity to teach their children about God's plan and purpose for the people of this world. The miraculous birth of baby Jesus, the crucifixion and death of our Lord and Savior, and the victorious resurrection of Jesus Christ are stories that can be told over and over again as these special holidays are celebrated year after year.

As a Christian parent, I often struggled with whether or not to incorporate secular celebrations into these deeply spiritual events. But I also realized that kids need to be kids, and imagination and fantasy are a critical part of childhood development. (Besides, how could I tell Mr. and Mrs. Santa they weren't welcome in our home?)

During my years as a stay-at-home mom, I listened to *Focus on the Family* almost every day. My husband and I attended James Dobson's video series and read many of his books—he literally helped us raise our children. I was even tempted to invite him

A Mom's Guide to Making Memories Last

to the high school graduation ceremonies! I remember one time when he was talking about celebrating Easter with his family. He said that they had an Easter egg hunt on Saturday and celebrated the true meaning of Easter on Easter Sunday. This idea appealed to me. Some Christians may disagree on this approach, and that's fine. The key is to find the right balance. As Christian parents, we must emphasize the spiritual significance of religious holidays and teach our children the truths of Scripture. Yet we can also allow our children to celebrate in age-appropriate ways, and record those celebrations in their journals. So whether you make Easter baskets for your kids, have egg hunts in the backyard, or color Easter eggs together, be sure to reserve Easter Sunday

Record What Defies Description

When my kids were in elementary school, Good Friday and Easter often fell during spring vacation, when we were rarely at home. As a result, many of our Easter observances have occurred in unfamiliar but unique places.

One year we were visiting friends in Colorado and attended an outdoor Easter morning service. The service began with a soloist belting out "Amazing Grace" on the saxophone. The clear blue skies above and the Rocky Mountains as a backdrop provided a majestic atmosphere impossible to describe further with words. I noted this in my kids' journals, knowing their own mental snapshots of the moment would remain in memory with that little reminder.

When my boys were grown and only Teri remained under our roof, Bob and I took her to Mexico for spring break. On Easter Sunday we followed a narrow dirt road that led to a tiny chapel in town. We sat in the back row with other spring breakers and listened as the pastor's wife translated into English what her dear husband was preaching in the native tongue. We shared communion with brothers and sisters in Christ and worshiped with music that transcended all cultures and languages. This was another Easter service experience that was difficult to express with words, yet it i recorded in Teri's journal so she will recall the experience in her own way in the yea to come.

for worship and for celebrating the victorious resurrection of our Savior, Jesus Christ.

Establish Traditions throughout the Year

The possibilities for family traditions are endless. If you've not established traditions of your own already, just know it's never too late to start:

- Plan a family night once a week when you can watch videos together or play board games.
- Let your kids eat breakfast in their pajamas while watching Saturday morning cartoons.
- Take walks together on Sunday afternoons.
- Decorate cookies on Valentine's Day.
- Make a special breakfast together every Memorial Day.

Traditions don't have to be expensive or time-consuming to be memorable. They're simply this: simple pleasures repeated. Embrace and enjoy them, and remind your children that these traditions are what make your family special.

Collect Holiday Books

Publishing companies know how families enjoy holiday books, so they continue to publish beautiful, seasonal volumes—some classics, some new—every Thanksgiving, Christmas, Easter, and Valentine's Day.

You can start your own holiday story collection by adding just one or two new editions to your library each year. Some books may be light and humorous, and others may be deeply spiritual. Add some of each so you have a wide variety of holiday books. You can read the light and humorous titles for the pure joy of reading, and the books with Christian messages will help your children understand the true meanings of holidays while also instilling in them your values and beliefs.

Make Mealtime Memories

Since we all need to eat, and most of us love to eat, mealtime can easily be transformed into a time for traditions and memory making.

On Sunday mornings it was always easier to get the kids out of bed with the aroma of cinnamon rolls engulfing the kitchen. Thanks to the Pillsbury Doughboy, that feat wasn't difficult to

Write Your Own Books— and Create a Keepsake

Reading books to my children was a daily routine we all enjoyed. But my kids also loved it when I made up my own stories. The words "once upon a time" can get the creative juices flowing and set anyone's imagination in high gear. Try making up a story for your kids and let them add to the story if they desire. You may want to write it down as you go so you can create your own publication. When you have finished the story, get out the crayons and let your kids be the illustrators. Whatever the result, you will have created a wonderful memory and keepsake—with lots of fun along the way.

achieve. After wiping icing off our lips, we headed to church and always returned home with hearty appetites. At Sunday noon we gathered around the dining room table to enjoy a full-course dinner: salad, meat, potatoes, and of course, dessert.

On Sunday night it was always pizza for dinner—frozen or takeout, since the kitchen was "closed."

These "Sunday specials" became family traditions, because we enjoyed them week after week, year after year; now that my kids are grown, these simple Sunday traditions have become pleasant memories.

Another favorite meal is our Christmas Day breakfast. After opening presents, and still wearing our pajamas, we always gather around the dining room table for homemade waffles, sausage, eggnog, and unhurried conversation. It's a time to be thankful for our family, our many blessings, and the gift of God's Son.

Easter, Thanksgiving, Christmas, and even the summer holidays are times when food plays an important part in our celebrations. From stuffed turkey and pumpkin pie to hot dogs on the grill, family memories are made as we share food and fellowship.

> The important thing to remember about traditional family feasts is that it's not the time, expense, or effort that goes into the planning and preparation but the consistency of repeating the family favorites.

Create a Family Cookbook

You can create a family treasure by copying into a notebook your family's favorite traditional feasting recipes.

Choose a notebook (perhaps with loose-leaf pages) that can be easily copied. For an extra personal touch, handwrite all the recipes or add special "cook's notes" at the end of every recipe ("This is John's favorite dish, so I always made it for his birthday").

Let family members add their favorite recipes to the family cookbook for several years. Then make copies for each person and give it to him or her for a special gift.

Your kids will thank you, especially when they move into homes of their own and can't remember that one special ingredient you always added to the Labor Day chili. They need not fear—the family cookbook's here with all your traditional foods in one handy volume sure to become a keepsake for generations to come.

Praying Together

Establish daily routines of praying together at mealtime, bedtime, or both. Many families hold hands around the table as they ask for God's blessing and thank him for their food. If you start this tradition when your children are young, they'll be comfortable doing it as teenagers, and it may remain their practice as adults. Praying with your children at bedtime is also something that can continue into the teen years.

Having your children recite short, memorized prayers is a good way to teach little ones to pray, and the practice reinforces how prayer is an important part of our everyday lives. But as kids get older, I believe they need to be encouraged to pray with their own words, knowing that prayer is simply talking to God. When children see that they can bring any need and concern to God, they develop a personal relationship with him and learn to trust in him. Praying for specific needs also allows our children to grow in their faith as they see God answer their prayers and learn to wait for his perfect timing and will to be accomplished.

Family Bible Reading and Devotion Times

When it comes to reading the Bible or having devotions together, be sure to keep materials age appropriate, meaningful, and enjoyable. It's easy to get into a rut and have devotions become a mundane ritual. Fresh ideas and variety will keep things interesting. You'll find all kinds of resources at your Christian bookstore—from Bibles for toddlers to devotions for teenagers.

When our children were very young, we used Bibles designed especially for their age groups, and these featured lots of pictures. As the children grew, we read from a family devotion book that offered a contemporary story, a Scripture verse, and a prayer.

A Prayer Cup for Thirsty Souls

Here's a fun way to teach children the importance of praying for others: Pass around a prayer cup that contains pieces of paper with names on them. Each person at the table draws one slip of paper, then prays for the person noted there.

Our children loved this idea and were always excited to see whose name they would pick: Grandpa, Grandma, the pastor, the next door neighbor—we added names as we continued the practice. It was a fun way to remember others in our family prayers.

You might try this and keep a log or journal of prayers and how God answered those prayers over time.

One thing my kids really enjoyed was something we called "Wisdom Search." My husband or I would read two or three verses from Proverbs (we chose the verses ahead of time), then specifically discuss how to apply the truths to everyday life. Sometimes our discussions were short and ended promptly, but many times we found ourselves in deep discussion about important issues.

Many of today's family devotionals offer discussion questions that may spark some meaningful conversations at the table. Don't be afraid to take a few risks and discover what works for your family.

Secret Pals

February in Michigan is not a really exciting month. The mixture of ice, snow, and cloudy days makes this shortest month of the year seem like the longest. But my kids always loved Valentine's Day, and we turned this day of love into a week of kindness.

One week prior to Valentine's Day, we drew names to acquire a secret pal. Then throughout the week the mission was to bestow secret acts of kindness on our pals: make his bed while he's in the shower, place an encouraging note in her coat pocket or a place she's sure to find it, or leave a small gift (handmade or just a piece of candy) on his pillow. When Valentine's Day arrived, we gave our secret pals Valentines to reveal our identities.

It was fun to have the whole family involved, and it was a great way to teach our children that we can show love through our actions. The biggest challenge was keeping our secret pals a secret! There were times when some of us would trade secret pals halfway through the week to create more mystery and confusion. But whether or not we figured out who our secret pals were, our Valentine week was always a week of kindness, fun, and happy memories. (Note: This is something you can do any time of the year.)

Shopping Trips

Whether it's a weekly trip to the grocery store or an annual gift-buying excursion, traditions can be added to the ritual of your shopping trips. Remember, traditions are just things you do over and over again, turning the mundane into something special by the way you do it. Here are some of our special memories:

- **Selecting a goody from the bakery at the grocery store first thing every shopping excursion**—This was a treat and kept the kids occupied, savoring their pastries, while I shopped. (My kids usually selected chocolate éclairs, but I chose a bagel since it was kinder to my thighs!)

- **Letting the kids choose one food item to put into the cart as we grocery shopped**—This gave them a special mission and kept them from asking for everything they saw.

- **Birthday shopping with Grandma**—Since our boys' birthdays are close together, Grandma would take both of them to the toy store each year to pick out their gifts. Now that my boys are grown, they may not remember every gift they selected, but they always remember the special shopping and memory-making times with Grandma.

Celebrating Birthdays

Children love celebrating their birthdays, because it's the one day of the year when they feel like the most important person in the world. Birthdays provide a great opportunity for family traditions to be created and continued through the years.

We have a china dinner plate that says, "You Are Special," and only the birthday person gets to use the plate on his or her birthday.

We also had a tradition of allowing our children to skip school on their birthdays and spend the day with Dad. They could spend the day however they wished as long as it was something they could do in one day without getting on an airplane.

My kids all have winter birthdays, so some years they chose indoor activities, while other years they went sledding or skiing at a local resort. No matter how they planned on spending their day, they always looked forward to their birthdays with Dad and thought we were pretty cool to let them play hooky!

Making a Tribute

A few months before my mother was to celebrate her eightieth birthday, my sisters and I began discussing what kind of special gift to give her. She didn't need another sweater, purse, or bottle of cologne, and her jewelry box was full of gifts from previous birthdays.

We decided to invite all of her children, their spouses, and her grandchildren to write a tribute to her, every person sharing a favorite memory or thanking her for something she'd done.

Twenty different family members contributed, and each tribute was humorous, poignant, spiritual, meaningful, and deeply emotional. We added past-and-present photographs of every contributor and assembled all the pieces in a memories album that cost less than thirty dollars.

When we presented the album to Mother, it was with her very own box of Kleenex; even today the album sits on her coffee table in the living room. That collection of tributes remains a testament to the love and affection we have for Mother, something she can enjoy anytime, over and over again.

Mother's Day, Father's Day, birthdays, or anniversaries are great opportunities to let our parents, grandparents, or other loved ones know how much they're loved and appreciated. And tribute albums don't take a lot of money—just some time, attention, and love—but remain priceless.

Shortcuts

All in One: Rather than keep a separate journal for each of the holidays, you may choose to keep one general special occasion journal where you document all holidays throughout the year. From New Year's Day in January to Christmas in December, you can write a brief blurb on how you celebrated and what you loved best.

The Calendar Journal: Buy a calendar that you use only for the purpose of journaling family events. (Use another calendar for everyday business like doctor's appointments, school activities, get-togethers, and such.) Write a sentence or two in the space provided on the specific date that you celebrated a holiday or special family tradition. At the end of each year, store these keepsake calendars in a drawer or box so they're like a historical log of the years behind you.

3

keep the adventures

Family Vacations and Special Events

Whether you travel by car, plane, boat, or train, a family vacation is always worth remembering. And whether your adventure is a day, a week, or an extended period of time, you'll be grateful years later if you document and preserve your experiences.

Whenever we go on a vacation, I always pack a journal—nothing fancy or expensive, just a colorful, compact notebook with empty pages begging to be filled.

Here's the good news—you have time to write on vacation and lots to write about! New surroundings, fun activities, and no distractions of everyday life at home provide you with the perfect opportunity to collect great family memories. You can also make your vacation journal a family affair by allowing everyone to contribute something at the end of each day.

happy trails and great adventures

One summer Bob was able to get a month off from work. We rented a van, locked our doors in Michigan, and headed down the Southeast Trail. Since both of our boys enjoyed playing tennis, we signed them up to play tournaments in the towns where we would be stopping.

From Kentucky to Georgia, our experiences were numerous and memorable. We rode horses and ate grits in Lexington, Kentucky. In Gatlinburg, Tennessee, Rob's tennis match was interrupted by a copperhead snake that slithered onto the court to get a better view of the game. In Hickory, North Carolina, we were starving but could find only restaurants with long waiting lines before settling for a takeout pizza. (What a memory as we sat on a curb in the parking lot to enjoy that mouth-watering meal.) In Lake City, South Carolina, the town was celebrating an annual tobacco festival, and we met the mayor, who invited us to join him for the pig roast at town hall. In Atlanta, Georgia, we visited Coca-Cola World and tasted all their soda flavors from all over the world until our stomachs were fully carbonated.

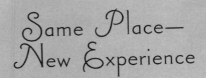

Same Place— New Experience

My friend Vicki and her family are expert campers who spend their summer weekends at a favorite spot just an hour from home. Most weekends it's the same routine: cooking on a camp stove, riding bikes, and fishing in the lake.

That is, till the weekend Vicki's daughter got tangled in an extension cord and tipped over a pot of boiling water on her bare foot. The next night Vicki's son tripped over a bike in the dark and cut his head. The following day the other son got a fishhook caught in his eyelid when his friend was casting a line into the lake.

During their three-day vacation, they made two trips to the emergency room. It was a weekend camping trip no one could have predicted—and no one will forget!

After all the adventure, we looked forward to getting back to the routine in Michigan. Our excitement wasn't over once we brought in the last suitcase though. We quickly discovered that a mother mouse and her babies had moved into our family room while we were away.

Home sweet home? Even the critters think so.

turning detours into delight

I once heard a speaker say, "If you want a time of family bonding, take a vacation—not because you'll have a wonderful time, but because something disastrous usually happens and it's the disaster that creates family bonding!"

How true. Think about it. Have you ever gotten lost while traveling or taken a wrong turn? Have you been stranded in an airport for several hours or even days? Did that luxury suite you reserved turn out to be a flea-infested room the size of a closet? These can be the parts of a trip that you remember the most, or at least don't easily forget.

Once in California Bob and the boys took a wrong turn after leaving a football game and ended up in a very scary part of town. They didn't dare stop to ask for directions, so they kept driving around until they finally found a road that led them to safety.

The scars have healed and the doctor bills have been paid, but to this day Vicki prefers the camping trips that follow the same old routine.

In Utah Rob came down with the chicken pox the day before we traveled home from a ski trip—and I sustained a cut, swollen lip after getting whacked in the mouth with a ski pole.

On a family trip to Alaska celebrating our twenty-fifth wedding anniversary, our hotel sent us to a place called Rent-A-Heap. I thought the name was clever until I realized it literally was a place to rent . . . a . . . heap! The only vehicle available was an old white pickup truck with a cracked windshield. All five of us packed ourselves into the truck and traveled for hours on Kodiak Island, down a narrow road that led to ocean streams, bald eagles, and wild animals. While the mode of transportation wasn't what we would have chosen, our experience in the white pickup truck turned out to be remarkable.

Think of the stories you can tell because of the unexpected, from dumpy motel rooms and long airport layovers to travels through towns not on the itinerary and emergency shopping trips when luggage is lost. Detours always give you a new perspective, even if only to make you more grateful for the roads usually traveled. That's something worth talking about.

great getaways nearby

Because of the pressures of our society and today's extravagant lifestyles, many parents feel the need to save their paychecks for several years in order to take their kids on a great vacation.

A mom once shared with me that she and her husband saved their money for three years so that they could finally afford a trip

A Mom's Guide to Making Memories Last

to Disney World. Though they had a great time on their vacation, their seven-year-old son was more interested in catching lizards than in seeing Mickey Mouse or going on a roller-coaster ride. He spent most of his time chasing lizards with an empty cup while the rest of the family stood in long lines waiting for a three-minute ride.

The truth is, your kids probably won't remember or appreciate the amount of money you spend on them. What they will remember, however, is the amount of *time* you spend with them. Going for bike rides, playing in the park, and visiting a zoo can become great memories for your children.

You don't need to travel great distances to get good respites and adventures. Many families spend their vacation days at nearby hotels, cottages, or campgrounds and still have adventure stories to tell. Catching minnows, exploring hiking trails, and roasting marshmallows are worth recording and remembering too, whether they happen on a mountaintop or right in your own backyard.

So rethink the time you believe you need to make a memory. Begin thinking about how a short weekend or even an afternoon spent with your children can be filled with special moments. Amazing things can happen when you try this.

One particular summer when our lives were busy with my boys' athletic activities, I sensed that Teri needed a little extra attention. So we took an afternoon—just the two of us—and went to the local zoo. We strolled the park leisurely, enjoying the animals and observing their interesting, often humorous behavior. We watched a mama bear snuggle with her cub in an open cave. We laughed

We often ignore the convenient and affordable opportunities right under our noses because we don't think of local activities as exciting enough. Think again, and take advantage of the tourist attractions in your own town or nearby.

- Visit your local museums.
- Spend a few hours in art galleries.
- Browse antique shops (when the kids are old enough!).
- Go for an afternoon drive or bicycle ride on country roads with no particular destination in mind—see where you end up.
- Take the train to the next town and back.

at the monkeys as they teased each other and swung freely from the tree limbs like professional trapeze artists. Our favorite stop was the prairie dog playground, where the adorable furry critters poked their heads out of tunnels and dug into new territory. Although we only spent a few hours together, that simple trip, just across town, remains one of Teri's favorite memories.

Another afternoon to remember occurred one snowy Saturday in February. Our family was housebound due to a harsh Michigan blizzard. Mountains of snow formed around our doors and windows until we began to feel somewhat claustrophobic. Bob and the boys decided to conquer the rugged outdoors and go on a winter expedition in our backyard woods.

Dressed in winter gear from head to toe, the three of them trekked through the snow with a backpack full of snacks and a thermos of hot chocolate. The trip didn't require an airplane ticket, a tank of gas, or time away from work, but the memory of that winter expedition is priceless.

The Dividends
of Undivided Attention

You don't have to go far away in order to spend quality time with one of your children. A Saturday morning breakfast at a quaint restaurant or a Sunday afternoon walk can provide a few hours of uninterrupted time and meaningful conversation between you and your child. If you can't get away for an extended period, make the most of the time you have to zero in on one of your children, giving him or her your undivided attention. It will be a worthwhile investment in your relationship as well as a sweet moment to remember.

one-on-one

As your children get older, you or your spouse might have the opportunity to take a trip with only one child rather than with the whole family. We've enjoyed many vacations as a family, but we've also had wonderful experiences spending time as parent and child, one-on-one.

Bob and Teri are the die-hard shoppers in our family. Whenever I go along, I usually wimp out after an hour or two, while they're just getting warmed up. Let me explain here that shopping and buying are not the same thing. When I go to the store, it's to buy something I need. If I find what I need at a good price, I buy it and bring it home, end of story. When Bob and Teri head to the store, they go *shopping*, which means they search the racks and shelves for hours and hours, looking for . . . who knows what . . . until they find the best bargain of the century.

When Teri turned sixteen, both of our boys were away at college. She loves anything that's downtown, so Bob took her to New York City for her birthday—just the two of them. They left the wimp at home. They not only went *shopping*, they also went to a musical and took in all the sights and sounds of New York City in December. It was a birthday Teri will never forget and a wonderful time of father-daughter bonding.

mission trips

Almost everyone who's gone on a mission trip starts off hoping to change the lives of people at the destination, but they come home knowing that their very own lives have changed too.

Bob has made several trips to remote villages in Honduras and Mexico with medical mission teams. When Scott was a junior in high school, he was able to miss a week of school and go along to Honduras. Though Bob's the dentist, Scott was asked to help pull teeth, assist in surgeries, use his Spanish, and witness firsthand the desolate life of families in a Third World country.

Our son returned with spiritual and emotional maturity and deeper appreciation for his everyday privileges—things we might never have taught with as much power here at home.

Our daughter learned these lessons on a mission trip too. The summer between Teri's sophomore and junior years of high school, she and I joined a women's team from our church and spent twelve days in Albania. We visited children in the orphanage, took them on outings to the seashore, and taught Bible school at a small church in

You don't have to travel to Third World countries to find needy people. From Indian reservations in New Mexico to inner city programs in New York, there are people and communities in need of physical things like food, shelter, clothing, and clean water. There are spiritual needs all around us too.

Reach out to others near and far, and you'll be enriched with memories and insights.

And consider going on a family mission trip—it could be the most meaningful adventure you ever take.

the village. Children of all ages walked to the church each day, eager to sings songs, listen to Bible stories, and receive a warm hug. All of us on the mission team fell in love with the people and sobbed when we had to say good-bye. Since our church sends a mission team every summer, we've been able to stay in touch with the friends we made—and I'm not sure who blesses whom more.

the more, the merrier

It's important that we spend time alone as a family to create family memories and strengthen our relationships with each other, but taking a vacation with other families or relatives can also be a positive experience. Having Grandpa or Grandma come along can be a tremendous help if your children are young, since extra adult hands are always appreciated. It also gives Grandpa and Grandma a chance to enjoy your children without the full responsibility they have when babysitting.

There are times when vacationing with another family or two can add fun to your experiences. Vacations at campgrounds and amusement parks are often more enjoyable when you share the experience with another family. Children can enjoy having play-mates, while you and your husband can enjoy the company of other adults.

My friend Dotty grew up in a family with five children and a mother who was a young widow. Every summer they joined a few other families for a serious camping trip. The hard work that was necessary to make these trips possible was much more enjoyable because it was shared by all, and it gave Dotty's mom the oppor-tunity to travel with other adults.

For families on a tight budget, renting a cottage or cabin with another family can make the trip affordable and allow them to enjoy a vacation they couldn't otherwise have taken. Obviously, this is an idea that can be a disaster if you choose to vacation with the wrong family—make sure you know your fellow travelers well before making your plans!

Ask for Autographs

Keep an interesting-people journal, or start an autograph book for the interesting folks you meet. You will soon begin to see what an amazing world this is—how God has created such variety, breadth, and depth in personalities and persons!

interesting people

No matter where your family's travels take you, you're sure to meet interesting people along the way. One year, at the Rose Parade in Pasadena, we met Harold, a fun, outgoing guy who had been protecting his front-row spot for nearly fifteen hours. For some reason, he finally decided to share his coveted territory with us. It may have been the coffee and doughnuts we offered, but he was kind to us nonetheless.

Now, we didn't know much about Harold, but it didn't take but a few minutes to watch a little drama unfold. One of the parade officials had asked him to guard a medium-sized cardboard box, which he agreed to do. As the parade began, Harold figured the box was forgotten and the official who left it in his charge wouldn't be coming back for it. So Harold opened the box and discovered dozens and dozens of folded T-shirts.

Remaining true to his generous spirit, Harold began passing out the T-shirts to folks around him. "Have a free T-shirt!" he exclaimed with glee as he randomly gave them away. As the passing floats began to steal his attention, Harold closed the box, which still contained a healthy supply of shirts.

A while later the official returned and asked Harold for the box. He promptly handed it to her, seeming relieved when she walked away without checking the contents. His expression changed to horror, though, as she turned back with the box under one arm and a T-shirt draped over the other.

"Is there a problem here?" he asked nervously.

"I forgot to thank you," the official said. "Here, have a T-shirt!"

My kids witnessed the whole incident and laughed until their sides ached. Though I had to explain to them later that what Harold did was wrong, I think they enjoyed watching him and his antics more than the parade!

I can think of so many fun, or at least interesting or famous, people we've met at hotels, restaurants, airports, ski lifts, and street corners. Bob and Rob had their picture taken with George H. W. Bush and Chris Everett at a fishing tournament in the Florida Keys; in a restaurant in Mexico, Bob, Teri, and I sat at a table that was right next to Mr. and Mrs. Bill Gates. We've also had lengthy chats with CEOs who traded their white-collar careers for art-fair exhibits, and then there's the middle-aged restaurant owner in Cabo San Lucas, Mexico, who came down for spring break when he was in college and never went back home. In Florida we fished with a guide who was formerly a police officer. At a hotel in Calgary, my kids got acquainted with an entire girls' soccer team (we went to their game the next morning), and in Chicago we shared breakfast with a man who lived on the streets.

The world is full of amazing people. Look for them and you'll be amazed. You'll find memorable experiences, and you just might make a new friend.

⚬ Shortcuts ⚬

Postcards: For an easy and inexpensive vacation journal, collect postcards as you travel, jot memories on them, and even mail a few of them home. Most of the towns you travel through will have gift shops with dozens of postcards. Almost everything you see as you travel, from scenic landscapes to historical monuments, can be found on a postcard—and the kids will love participating. By the time you return home, the details of your trip will be well preserved.

Photo Journaling: If you take a lot of pictures on vacation, arrange them in an album, note the dates and locations, and write a sentence or two about each picture. The sooner you get your pictures developed and organized, the more details you'll remember about your trip.

Guest Book: If you own a cottage, cabin, or home with a swimming pool, you probably get lots of company. Keep a guest book in your foyer and have your guests sign and date the book. Many folks will add interesting little notes about their visit. See? The journaling can be done for you!

Program Covers and Ticket Stubs: Attending concerts, plays, and sporting events as a family can be great fun. Save the ticket stubs or program covers in an album or special box to jog memories. These items usually include the date and event, so little or no writing is necessary.

4

just for you

When Teri was six years old, she sang in the children's choir at church. Since there were a lot of kids in the choir, the parents were asked to take turns sitting among the children to keep them attentive.

Once when I was taking my turn to chaperone, the director was teaching the kids a new song. The little boy sitting next to me was singing his heart out as if he already knew every note and every word.

He admitted he didn't know the song, but his answer surprised me when I asked, "How did you learn that so fast?"

"I don't have very much in my brain yet!" he exclaimed.

Such truth out of the mouths of babes.

Truly, moms have very busy lives, and their brains, just like their schedules, are filled with household chores, carpooling, family commitments, volunteer involvement, careers, and more—too much to do and remember. It's no wonder we have little room left for being creative or learning a new song!

Well, moms, this is where journaling comes in. Journaling helps sort and unclutter what's in our minds. It can help us make sense of yesterday and today. It's like therapy that helps you discern, a best friend who encourages and supports, a cup of coffee that gives you new energy or a jolt, a soothing compress that relieves an aching temple—and a beautiful treasure box holding all the things most dear to us that we want to remember, every note and every word.

The practice of journaling is the way to learn a new song.

private—keep out!

Everyone needs a safe, private place to bare his or her soul and sort out his or her thoughts and feelings. When I was a teenager, I had a personal diary. I kept it in the drawer of a small desk in my bedroom, where I did most of my studying. In one drawer was my white diary, some important papers, and my appointment cards; hidden away in another drawer was the key that opened and closed my diary's little lock.

I loved that diary and confided in it my joys, heartaches, and embarrassing moments. The lined pages offered me the opportunity to write whatever secret information I wanted to record. It held stories of best friends and new crushes, slumber parties and basketball games.

Writing in a personal diary or journal is more than just recording facts. It's an opportunity to write from your heart and soul as you reflect on the events, circumstances, and people in your life.

I was blessed with a wonderful God-fearing family, was loved and cared for, and was taught the Scriptures from the day I was born. But even the best family in the world cannot protect a child from every emotional issue. I was always small for my age—and very skinny. I had some health issues that I struggled with, and I was socially immature. Though I made friends easily, I didn't always fit in with the crowd and often felt like a tagalong. These were issues I didn't know how to discuss with those around me, but I could write about my thoughts and emotions in my diary.

Somehow, by holding a pen in my hand, I could form words that allowed me to reach into my soul and pull out what was deep inside. After all the words were poured onto the pages, I could close the book and turn the lock so no one would know.

Recess Queen

When I was in sixth grade, my favorite time was recess, because I was the queen of double-Dutch jump rope. I could jump longer and faster than anyone else in my grade. (Since I was a scrawny kid, this was a huge boost to my self-esteem!) On the first day of seventh grade, I walked to school wearing my best pair of tennis shoes, eager to rule the ropes once again. When I arrived at school, however, I noticed that most of the girls were wearing nylons and loafers, and I wondered how they planned on jumping rope at noon recess. Well, let me put it this way: they didn't! They all stood around in small clusters, giggling about boys and whispering about things like periods and bras (to which I could not relate!). My peers had turned into teenagers over the summer, and I was still a girl. I joined one of the clusters and listened to girl talk, but I would have rather been jumping.

As adult women, we deal with emotional issues from day to day.

Our children exhaust us.

Our husbands hurt us.

Our friends disappoint us.

We might not feel like discussing these matters with anyone—maybe because we don't even know how to begin.

We can hold pens in our hands though. We can form words on a page in a book that we can open and close and keep in a private drawer. Let these ideas and suggestions help you reach in and pull out what's deep inside your soul.

becoming a mom

When I was speaking at a women's conference, a woman shared that she wrote in a journal during her pregnancy because she wanted to remember all the details that are so easily forgotten once the baby is born. The first sign of a heartbeat, the first kick, the first

Speedy Delivery

Though each of my three pregnancies and deliveries were incredible, memorable events, delivering Scott was probably the most dramatic. After several nights of interrupted sleep due to false labor, I awoke once again to some fairly strong contractions. I woke up Bob (once again!) and told him we should go to the hospital. He suggested I go back to sleep.

After a trip to the bathroom, I noticed that I had started bleeding and convinced Bob it was time to go. We called Bob's parents at 3:00 a.m. to let them know we were bringing three-year-old Rob to their house on the way to the hospital. As I panted through the contractions that were getting stronger and closer together, Bob explained to sleepy-eyed Rob that he was about to be a big brother.

"We need to go!" I said sternly as Bob chatted with his parents in the foyer. As we waved good-bye and got into the car, heads of sweat formed on my forehead contraction—all of these moments created a flood of emotions that she expressed in her own personal journal so she could remember them forever.

If you've ever been pregnant, then you have an exciting story to tell.

Even if your pregnancy happened years ago, you may still recall many of the details with a little thought and reflection.

- Did you get pregnant right away, or did it take years of doctor's appointments and temperature charts?
- Did you endure morning sickness?
- Were you plagued by frequent potty stops?
- How about kicks to your ribs—was your growing, developing baby active in the womb?

Every pregnant woman also has her own story of labor and delivery. Some women spend countless hours pushing and panting, while others give birth in the elevator. Some women have C-

(did I mention it was February?). We were finally on our way to the hospital when Bob did the unthinkable—he stopped for a red light.

"It's 3:30 in the morning!" I hollered at the top of my lungs. "There are no cars in sight. For Pete's sake, keep going!"

Finally we were at the hospital, and it seemed to me like everyone was moving in slow motion. "Can you give me a urine sample?" a kind orderly asked. "Maybe when my contractions stop,"

I answered in a not-so-kind voice. As I squatted over the toilet to produce the requested sample, I felt an urge to push. "I'm pushing!" I hollered through the bathroom door. I had no idea how those two words would send the maternity staff into fast-forward motion.

Scott was born at 4:20 a.m. just as Bob entered the delivery room. "Wow, that was easy!" said Bob with a look of delight.

Thank goodness for my journal—so I could write my own version of this "easy" delivery.

sections in a sterile room, while others deliver at home. Whatever your story, you can tell it in your own words and style to share with your children or to keep for yourself.

Maybe you never experienced pregnancy and childbirth. If your children are adopted or you married a man with children, you still have some very special stories of your own.

I have several friends who have children who are adopted, and each of their stories is unique and wonderful. Some of these children came from teenage moms who weren't ready to be parents, while others came from orphanages in foreign countries. It's always amazing to see how God unfolds his plan for a family and places children in the arms of the right parents.

No matter how you did it, becoming a mom is an amazing story worth recording.

raising kids—and the roof

I think most moms would agree that raising children is the most rewarding experience a woman can have—and the quickest way to drive us crazy. Our days are filled with priceless moments like first steps, first words, warm hugs, and sticky kisses. But our days can also be filled with hair pulling, teasing, screaming, and muddy shoes.

I confess there are times when I've lost control of my temper and yelled at my kids. "Do what I say and do it now!"—a command that could shatter windows with the decibel level at which it was delivered. Though it can feel great to let off steam, we all know there are better ways to release frustration (running around the block can help, but then you always have to come back . . .).

Have you ever tried writing away your frustrations?

It really does work. In fact, it can feel just as good as yelling at the kids, because you release things into the open—and because your journal can't talk back to you or give you advice. It's just there for you to vent and fume or do whatever you need to do.

While these are pages you may choose to tear up and toss away the next day, they're pages worth writing if they help for the moment.

creative conflict

I was recently at a book signing when a woman sharply criticized one of my books in front of me and some other women. Since this had never happened to me in my twelve years of writing, speaking, and book signing, I was shocked. I didn't know how to respond. The incident happened so quickly that I just sat there with my eyes bulging and my blood pressure rising.

I managed to utter a few words in self-defense, but I quickly learned it's futile to argue with an angry person. Another woman who heard the attack explained to me why this woman responded

Every mother has a story to tell.

○ Journal to Get It All Out—and Let It Go ○

If you have a child who struggles socially, emotionally, or academically, you know how his or her struggles become yours too. Find relief, and possibly helpful insights, by recording specific incidences of your struggles, both positive and negative. This not only will help you process your emotions but may help you keep track of your child's progress or setbacks.

the way she did. It helped me understand the situation, but I was still hurting.

That night I typed a full-page letter to the woman, explaining how she was completely wrong in what she'd said. I defended all of my books, including the one she'd criticized, and presented several specific examples of how she was nothing but a big hypocrite. I also scolded her for having the nerve to humiliate me in public. After I let out my anger, I began to release my hurt.

It felt good to write the letter. The process helped my emotions to settle. My blood pressure stabilized, and my eyes went back into my head. Writing that letter was exactly what I needed to do to handle my emotions and deal with the conflict.

The next day I read the letter two or three times. It felt good to read it. I was proud of myself for expressing my words so beautifully and confidently. Then I tore up the letter and threw it away. I never had any intention of giving the letter to the woman. I wrote the letter for myself so I could work through the emotions, let go of the incident, and move on.

Not all conflict can be resolved in this way. Obviously, there are times when a two-way conversation is needed to reach a resolution. Some conflict may require the help of a professional counselor or pastor, but if you're having conflict with a friend, relative, or spouse, journaling about your problem may help you sort out the issues and see things more clearly. It may also help you release your emotions in a more positive way.

dwell on these things

Writing about frustrations, hurts, and disappointments can be a healthy emotional exercise, as it allows us to reflect, release, and let go. But it's important to dwell on our positive circumstances as well. If we write only about negative things, our writing will always have a negative focus. In Philippians 4:8 the apostle Paul reminds us, "Whatever is true, whatever is noble, whatever is right, whatever is pure, whatever is lovely, whatever is admirable—if anything is excellent or praiseworthy—think about such things."

If you are ever having a bad day (or even if you're not), get out your journal, list your blessings, and thank God for them. Include the following Scripture verse from Psalm 118:24: "This is the day

To keep your mind dwelling on things excellent and worthy of praise, make sure some of your journal entries include thanking God for the gifts, mercies, and blessings he showers upon us each day.

that the LORD has made; let us rejoice and be glad in it." Think about the good people you have in your life—the family members and friends who are there for you when you need them. Try to recall acts of kindness others have shown toward you, and look for things for which you can be thankful.

When I was three months pregnant with my second baby, I was feeling horrible every day. I was tired, nauseated, and irritable, plus I had a toddler to care for. I was also planning a bridal shower for my soon-to-be sister-in-law. The day before the shower, my mother-in-law, an aunt, and a friend from church came over to clean my house. They vacuumed, dusted, picked up toys, scrubbed sinks, and cleaned toilets. Even though I was struggling physically and emotionally, the kindness of these women changed my focus and gave me a reason to be thankful. When we count our blessings and reflect on God's goodness, our bad days aren't so bad after all.

One day I decided to count my blessings and write them down in the form of a poem:

Counting My Blessings

In counting my blessings
I needed to include:
clean air to breathe,
water and food,
children to teach,
babies to love,
a warm cozy house,
and angels above.

In counting my blessings
I must think of these:
a peaceful sunset,
a warm, gentle breeze,
a fresh summer rain,
a starlit night,
and strong little arms
that hug me so tight.

In counting my blessings
these will be there:
friends in my life,
and people that care,
places to worship,
freedom to pray,
and wisdom from God
day after day.

In counting my blessings
it's easy to see
that the Lord must care
very deeply for me.[4]

glimpses of inspiration

Every once in a while, something unexpected happens that catches us by surprise and brings a glimmer of hope or truth into our souls. I perceive these instances as divine inspiration—little reminders from God that he is beside me all the way.

For example, one winter evening I had followed our usual bedtime routine—read a few storybooks, say a prayer, and tuck Rob in bed.

A short while later as I walked by his bedroom, I noticed I'd forgotten to close the drapes. The full moon was aligned in such a way that a brilliant beam penetrated the window and cast a ray of light on Rob's bed like a spotlight from heaven. His little three-year-old body barely made a bump under the covers, and the sight of him lying in the moonlight was breathtaking.

The night was quiet and still, and I felt like God was saying to me, "Don't worry, I am watching over him." I was reminded of the passage from Psalm 121 where it says, "He who watches over you will not slumber; . . . The LORD watches over you—the LORD is your shade at your right hand; the sun will not harm you by day, nor the moon by night. The LORD will keep you from all harm—he will watch over your life" (vv. 3, 5–7).

This is journal material!

Life is full of little lessons from above if we pause long enough to absorb them. Psalm 46:10 says, "Be still, and know that I am God." If you ever have a moment when God speaks to you in a powerful way, write it down so you will never forget it.

tragedy and loss

My friend Nan had a beautiful teenage niece who died suddenly from a brain hemorrhage. Both Nan and her niece were Christians, but the grieving process was long and painful. Nan tried to go back to work and resume her regular activities, but she couldn't stop thinking about her niece. She was afraid that as time went on and life continued, it would be as if her niece had never existed.

Nan decided to buy a journal. In the journal Nan wrote about her niece. She wrote down everything she could remember from the day her niece was born until the day she died. She included some photos and a few other keepsakes, then placed the journal on a bookshelf. The journal didn't replace Nan's niece. The journal did not bring Nan's niece back to life. But the journal allowed Nan to preserve all the special memories she had of her niece so they would not be forgotten. Creating the journal allowed Nan to resume her normal life. She could go back to work and enjoy social activities, because she knew that any time she wanted to think about her niece, she could pull the journal from the shelf and reflect on her memories.

hopes and dreams

I've often heard that if you write down a goal, you are more likely to accomplish it. Writing a goal on paper makes it more than a dream. It becomes a reality worth pursuing and establishes a certain amount of accountability.

Keep a Loved One Near with Memories

If you lose a loved one, there's nothing in the world that can replace that person. But preserving that person's memory may help ease the pain and allow you to move forward without losing the special moments of the past. Try these memory-keeping practices:

- In a journal or notebook, write down your favorite moments with the person you lost. You could ask others who loved this person to add their favorite memories too. There is comfort and strength in knowing you are not alone in your grief.
- What were your lost one's favorite pastimes? Gardening? You can plant that person's favorite tree or perennial in a place where it can be attentively tended. Or you can paste a sprig, leaf, or bloom from his or her favorite tree in your journal with a letter of your grief. Did the one you lost love cooking? Why not make that person's favorite recipe and share it with others who loved him or her too? These nurturing testaments are acts of faith that life goes on and proclamations of belief that love goes on and never dies. In time these acts can help you see again: love can endure all things.
- Tuck a picture of the person you loved and lost inside the pages of your Bible, next to Psalm 56:8, which reminds us God is there for us in sorrow—he keeps our every tear in his bottle, in his book.

Several years ago Bob attended a business conference where he engaged in some in-depth self-evaluation by responding to a questionnaire. He had to evaluate his past accomplishments, present commitments, and future plans. The questionnaire also encouraged him to reveal his deepest dreams and desires. He learned a lot about himself through this questionnaire and felt it was a useful tool for

A Mom's Guide to Making Memories Last

his personal and spiritual life as well as his business life. He was able to get an extra copy of the questionnaire, and he handed it to me when he returned home.

I do not enjoy filling out forms or answering questionnaires, but I obeyed my dear husband's pleas and did it. By writing thoughtful answers to the questions, I discovered that I was satisfied with my accomplishments thus far but that I had a longing to write for children. I didn't know how, when, why, or where. I just wanted to write. Our youngest child was about to start school, and I would soon have a few quiet hours during the day to use for my own personal pleasure. I wanted to fill those hours with writing. When I shared my discovery with my husband, he answered, "Well, then you'd better write if that is what God put in your heart."

Psalm 37:4 says, "Delight yourself in the LORD and he will give you the desires of your heart." I believe that if we are truly seeking God's will for our lives, spending time in his Word, and being obedient, then the desires we have are from God.

The publishing world is challenging, scary, and mysterious. I had no clue where to begin except to just start writing. I wrote a few humorous poems for kids, and soon my collection of poems was more than a dozen. Two weeks after I openly expressed my desire to write for children, I received an offer to write lyrics for children's piano music. Three years later my first book was published, and ten years later I had nearly thirty books in print.

Moms, what are your hopes and dreams? Search your heart, ask for God's direction, and write them down on paper! When you identify your desires, you can move forward with confidence as God directs your path. I can't promise that your dreams will be fulfilled in two weeks or even two years. But I do believe that if you write down your hopes and dreams, pray about them, and set goals to accomplish them, they have a much greater chance of becoming a reality.

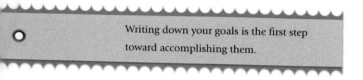

Writing down your goals is the first step toward accomplishing them.

days gone by

I'm often asked to speak on the topic of journaling because it is something many women are interested in, but they are not sure how to do it. After one of my sessions, a sweet great-grandmother came to me for advice. "My children and grandchildren want me to write about my life," she explained. "I'm eighty-three years old, and I don't know where to begin."

The thought of journaling eight decades of life is overwhelming for even the most gifted writers. It would be ideal if each of us began journaling when we were young and wrote in our journals regularly to keep them up-to-date. But for those of us who haven't done that, it's not too late.

If you want to reclaim and preserve your past, you can follow the advice I offered my senior friend. Do not try to write about your entire life all at once. Divide your life into decades, and begin

A Mom's Guide to Making Memories Last

with your earliest memories. The following questions may help bring back some of those memories.

Ages 0–20

Where were you born?

Where did you live?

Describe your house and your family.

Did you have any pets?

Where did you go to school?

Who were your friends?

Where did you go to church?

What were your favorite subjects, hobbies, or activities?

What special family events or traditions do you remember?

How did you celebrate your birthdays?

How did you celebrate Thanksgiving, Christmas, or other holidays?

Cold Feet

One of my earliest childhood memories goes back to when I was only four years old. My sister Karen and I were playing at a nearby creek on a winter afternoon, when we were tempted to walk on the semi-frozen surface. Karen bravely took two quick steps on the ice and made it safely across. As I followed her lead, I plunged through the thin ice and found myself in chilly waters. Though the water was no more than waist high, my boots were stuck in the muddy bottom, and Karen couldn't pull me out. A few moments later, my brother came by on this way home from school and helped me out of the creek. My mom was horrified when she saw my cold, wet body and frozen tears on my cheeks. After she gave me a warm bath, I put on my flannel pajamas, cuddled under a soft blanket, and fell asleep.

Use photos from albums or the good old shoe box and put them in chronological order. As you arrange the pictures in an album, include specific details or stories about the pictures.

Did you go on any trips or take vacations?

What were the difficult events of these decades?

What were the best events of these decades?

Ages 21–30

Where did you live?

Describe your home, family, and extended family.

What jobs did you have?

What degrees or titles did you earn?

Did you get married or have children?

What were your favorite hobbies or activities?

Did you travel anywhere?

Who were your closest friends?

What struggles or difficulties did you have?

How did God bless you during these years?

What were the best events of this decade?

Ages 31–50

Use any of the above questions to recall memories for each decade. If you remember a specific incident, write about it in the form of a story, including all the details you can remember.

Reclaim your past by writing a journal about your life.

prayer journals

Prayer is simply talking to God. We can talk to him just like a friend, and the great thing is, he's the best listener. He gives us his undivided attention all the time.

If you choose to write your prayers in a journal, you can write them in the same way—using everyday language as though you were talking to a friend and giving him your undivided attention.

I found out what a valuable tool this can be when one day I was home caring for my little ones (and experiencing a little PMS!). I was feeling completely overwhelmed with my responsibilities as a mother. Not only did I need to feed, clothe, bathe, protect, and nurture my children, but I was also responsible for their spiritual training. I questioned my ability to do all that was required of me, and I felt incompetent and inexperienced.

Then I remembered I didn't have to do it alone. I was blessed with a godly husband and extended family who supported me.

A wonderful benefit of keeping a prayer journal is how you can see the way God answers every heart cry over time. In times of doubt or trouble, your prayer journal also serves as a great source of encouragement, a safe place to pour out your hopes and fears, and a powerful reminder of God's love and faithfulness.

More than that, I had a heavenly Father who would watch over my kids day and night. God could be with my children when I wasn't there. He would be with them when I had to leave them with a babysitter or at the neighbor's house. And he would be with them on their first day of school when I said good-bye at the classroom door and sobbed all the way home.

After I processed all these thoughts, I sat down at my desk and wrote a prayer for God to be with my children. It was a way of releasing my children from my hands and placing them into his. Since I prefer to express myself in verse, this is what I wrote:

A Mother's Prayer

My gracious heavenly Father,
Please hear me as I pray.
I come to you on bended knee
And ask of you today,
To give me wisdom, strength, and love
To raise my children for you,
That they might love and honor you
In everything they do.

I ask that you'll watch over them
Throughout their childhood years.
Protect them as they run and play,
And calm their childish fears.
And when they reach their teenage years
I pray that they'll be strong,
To stand up to temptation
And turn away from wrong.
I pray that they would read your Word
And talk with you each day,
So they will know your perfect will
And follow in your way.
I ask that you would be their guide
As they begin to date.
Help them choose, dear Lord, I pray,
A loving, godly mate.

And when they're blessed with little ones
I pray that they may too
Have the wisdom, strength, and love
To raise their children for you.[5]

On one simple page, I poured out my heart to God. The matter was between him and me, and I kept it private for fifteen years. Some things are like that, and a prayer journal helped me ponder God's power and increase my faith.

There's an additional benefit: writing your prayers in a journal is a good way to keep balance in your prayer life. It's easy to run to God when you have a desperate need—and God certainly wants

Practicing Prayer on Paper

A young mom once shared with me that she found her personal quiet time very frustrating because it was never quiet, never a time of peace. The needs of her little ones kept interrupting.

In desperation, though, she found a solution. She found that if she wrote her prayers on paper, she could always go back to them after any interruption. After weeks of using this method, she realized she'd unwittingly started a prayer journal. This safe place to write out her most intimate conversations—the ones with her Creator and Savior—became so dear and important for her that she continued to write her prayers even after her kids were older and the interruptions less frequent.

you to come to him at those times. But as our Father, God also enjoys our praise and thanksgiving just as any mother enjoys glad chatter or thoughtful conversations with her children.

As you begin listing the things you're thankful for, you'll soon recognize your many blessings. Praise God for his greatness, power, and love. Let his nature lift you up and encourage you. Offer him your praise and gratitude; watch him fill you with hope and help to face even the most difficult challenges.

If you want to begin a prayer journal, here are a few tips:

- Choose a time of day when you may have a few moments to yourself. (If you have preschoolers at home, put on a VeggieTales video to offer them positive entertainment while you spend this "alone time" with God.)

- Put on the answering machine so you won't be interrupted by phone calls.
- Get out your prayer journal and pen, or use the computer.
- Start by writing praises to God for his greatness and love.
- List specific blessings in your life and thank God for these things.
- Confess anything that you need to confess on a separate page or piece of scrap paper. After you ask for forgiveness, tear it up and throw it away.
- Write your requests to God, pouring out your deepest needs, concerns, or fears.

(And remember, moms, if you don't finish in one sitting, pick it up where you left off at a later time.)

journaling scripture

Reading comprehension has never been one of my strengths. When I start reading, I can concentrate on the material for a while, but soon a part of my brain goes off in a different direction, and I think about other things. *What should I make for dinner? Maybe I could take that talk I need to give tomorrow in a different direction. Did I turn off my curling iron?* So to do well in school, I had to be a good note taker, because taking notes helped me concentrate more on the material at hand and remember what I'd read.

The same thing is true for me when it comes to reading the Bible.

If I just sit and read, the Scriptures don't sink in. But if I take a few notes as I'm reading, I understand more and remember it longer.

For example, one day I was reading about Jonah in the Old Testament. Jonah 2:8 caught my attention: "Those who cling to worthless idols forfeit the grace that could be theirs."

I wondered on the pages of my journal, *Is this verse saying that when we desire to hold on to possessions that have only earthly value (worthless idols), we're missing some of the things God has in store for us?*

If I'd simply read the verse and kept on reading, I probably would have soon forgotten it. But because the idea in the verse struck me and I wrestled with it on paper for a minute, that Scripture has stayed with me for years.

There's no doubt God speaks to us through his Word—and you can count on his messages always being personal and relevant.

Keep a notebook by your Bible. Whenever you read passages, write down in your own words what God is saying to you and how it applies to your life.

favorite Bible verses

A dear friend of mine gave me a cool journal for my birthday (the big five-oh), so I wanted to use it for something special. Over the decades I've memorized dozens of Bible verses that are a continual source of hope, comfort, and encouragement. The problem is, I can't remember where they're found, and it always takes a concordance search to find them. I decided to use the journal as my own personal collection of favorite Bible verses.

I divided the journal into the following sections: The Greatness of God; Forgiveness and Salvation; Hope and Comfort; Praise, Joy, and Thanksgiving; and Daily Living. All of my favorite verses are now in one place, and it is easy for me to find the verse I need when I need it. I can also add verses to the additional pages when I come across a verse I want to remember. I not only use the journal as a reference book but use it when I want to meditate on awesome verses. Here are a few examples:

The Greatness of God

For the LORD your God is God of gods and Lord of lords, the great God, mighty and awesome, who shows no partiality and accepts no bribes.

Deuteronomy 10:17

Yours, O LORD, is the greatness and the power
and the glory and the majesty and the splendor,
for everything in heaven and earth is yours.
Yours, O LORD, is the kingdom;
you are exalted as head over all.

1 Chronicles 29:11

How awesome is the LORD Most High,
the great King over all the earth!

Psalm 47:2

Forgiveness and Salvation

For as high as the heavens are above the earth,
so great is his love for those who fear him;
as far as the east is from the west,
so far has he removed our transgressions from us.

Psalm 103:11–12

For what I received I passed on to you as of first importance: that Christ died for our sins according to the Scriptures.

1 Corinthians 15:3

For it is by grace you have been saved, through faith—and this not from yourselves, it is the gift of God—not by works, so that no one can boast.

Ephesians 2:8–9

Hope and Comfort

Those who know your name will trust in you,
for you, Lord, have never forsaken those who seek you.

Psalm 9:10

God is our refuge and strength,
an ever-present help in trouble.

Psalm 46:1

Now to him who is able to do immeasurably more than all we ask or imagine, according to his power that is at work within us, to him be glory in the church and in Christ Jesus throughout all generations, for ever and ever! Amen.

Ephesians 3:20–21

Cast all your anxiety on him because he cares for you.

1 Peter 5:7

Praise, Joy, and Thanksgiving

> You have made known to me the path of life;
> you will fill me with joy in your presence,
> with eternal pleasures at your right hand.

Psalm 16:11

> I will praise you, O Lord my God, with all my heart;
> I will glorify your name forever.

Psalm 86:12

Be joyful always; pray continually; give thanks in all circumstances, for this is God's will for you in Christ Jesus.

1 Thessalonians 5:16–18

Daily Living

> Trust in the Lord with all your heart
> and lean not on your own understanding;
> in all your ways acknowledge him,
> and he will make your paths straight.

Proverbs 3:5–6

He has showed you, O man, what is good.

And what does the LORD require of you?

To act justly and to love mercy

and to walk humbly with your God.

Micah 6:8

Be very careful, then, how you live—not as unwise but as wise, making the most of every opportunity, because the days are evil. Therefore do not be foolish, but understand what the Lord's will is.

Ephesians 5:15–17

Therefore, as God's chosen people, holy and dearly loved, clothe yourselves with compassion, kindness, humility, gentleness and patience.

Colossians 3:12

Whether it's you talking to God or God talking to you, journaling on a spiritual level can deepen your relationship with your heavenly Father.

∘ Shortcuts ∘

If you're a busy mom (aren't we all?), writing in a personal journal may be the last thing crying "urgent" in your daily or weekly routine.

It doesn't have to be just one more thing for your to-do list that makes you groan. Try on these ideas for collecting memories:

- Create a computer file for your personal journal or prayers. Give yourself ten minutes to log a few entries each week. You can write a lot in ten minutes! Print the pages and put them in a binder. Voila! A journal that works for you.
- Keep a journal or small notebook by your bed so it's always nearby. Take a few minutes every now and then at the end of the day to jot down a few words. You can elaborate at a future time or just keep what you've written. Even a short entry will preserve special thoughts and memories.
- Collect wise words of others. As you come across tidbits of wisdom, sound advice, or gold nuggets of truth that speak to you, clip them and save them in a pretty box or scrapbook.

5

"thanks for the memories, mom"

Creative Ideas That Leave a Legacy of Love

When I was raising my children, I felt like I would be raising them for the rest of my life. I couldn't imagine a life without carpooling, packing lunches, biting my nails at tennis meets, screaming at hockey games, and attending parent-teacher conferences. I guess I knew in the back of my mind that someday my kids would grow up, but I didn't expect it to happen so quickly.

And then one morning I woke up and Rob was packing his bags for college. His bed was made, his toys were put away, and he was ready to leave the nest.

As we boarded the plane for Miami, I made small talk and tried to smile, but underneath the surface my heart ached, and I could hardly hold back the tears. I'd thought giving birth was painful, but it doesn't come close to the pain of standing on the sidewalk in front of your child's dormitory, giving him a hug and kiss good-bye, knowing it will be months until you see him again.

Two years later Scott packed his bags for college, and I thought this send-off from the nest just might be easier. I'd done this before. I knew what to expect, right? Scott was more independent than his siblings, and I'd had a lifetime with him knowing he was ready to be on his own.

Yet as I stood in front of another dormitory, this one in South Carolina, nothing could have prepared me for the pain of another good-bye.

Eventually I adjusted to having my boys in college and was thrilled when they came back for visits.

Then, on a Saturday morning in January, I found myself sitting on a front pew in a little chapel in the mountains of Pennsylvania. I couldn't believe the young man at the altar was the little boy I'd brought into the world. There he stood, holding the hands of his soul mate, declaring his love for the new woman in his life.

Rob was still my son, but now he was becoming a husband and would have a new permanent home.

My nest at home was beginning to empty. I was thankful that we still had several years left with Teri. But those years passed too quickly, and soon I was helping her squeeze almost everything she owned into suitcases and boxes (girls have more stuff than boys!). Bob and I flew with her to Texas and spent several days helping her move into her dormitory before we finally said good-bye to our baby.

It doesn't matter how often a parent goes through this process; your heart bleeds every time. There's joy in seeing your children mature into young adults with good morals and values—evidence, you tell yourself, that you must have done something right. But there's sadness in wishing you had more time and could keep them little for one more day.

Letting your children go is much more painful than bringing them into this world.

Part of the pain is that feeling every mother has: *If I'd known how quickly my kids were going to grow up, I would have changed the way I parented.* I still would have taught them the same things I wanted them to learn, and I still would have bandaged all the boo-boos and wiped their tears, but I would have done other things too, like chilled out more and not gotten so upset about what didn't matter. You know what I'm talking about: Dirty floors that can be washed. Messy rooms that can be straightened. Fingerprints that can be wiped away.

I used to joke about the fact that I would clean my house after my kids left home. Now that they're gone, it's not funny anymore.

A recent moment with a friend reminded me of this. My friend is a mother of three young children and smack-dab in the middle of those hectic, exhausting years. When I was at her house recently, I noticed dozens of pictures on her refrigerator. One was of her three-year-old son, his face covered with white powder. All you could make out in the photo were his two little eyes.

"Oh my!" I said, smiling. "What's this one all about?"

My friend paused, momentarily lost in the scene. "He was playing in the baby's nursery and decided to powder himself," she said.

I looked at the picture and shared her joy. *Such innocence,* I thought. *Such sweetness. Isn't it neat that she ran for the camera instead of the washcloth?*

Of course, all mothers have times when we lose our patience, and it's impossible to be a perfect mother. But now that my kids are grown, I wish I'd run for the camera more often than the washcloth.

The good news is that even when kids grow up, they are never really gone. They come home often, and a new relationship begins to form between the parent and adult child. They still come to you for advice, though they don't always choose to follow it.

One of my favorite times now is when we're all together and my kids start reminiscing about the past. They love to remind me of my poor parenting techniques—like the time I sent Scott to his room for two hours because he asked for some barbecue sauce at the dinner table, or the time I thought Teri was being lazy and we found out she had mono, or another time I disciplined Scott for something Teri had done. (Perhaps I should write a book on how *not* to raise children!) But fortunately, my kids also remember the good times and things we did together because we were a family and we loved one another.

I will forever cherish the wonderful family memories we've created throughout the years. Some of those memories resulted from planned activities, while others were purely spontaneous events that unfolded before our eyes. You can create and preserve treasured memories for your family too. It starts with one memory made and preserved, one more memory, and then another, until you have a lifetime of memories. All it requires is your attention and love.

do what you can

The following pages are chock-full of fun and simple ideas that I've gathered through the years from other moms and from my own experiences. Please remember that you cannot possibly do them all—just dip into these pages like you're going shopping. You may have to browse awhile until something catches your eye. Pick what you can spend time on now; come back for more later.

You'll want to try on a few ideas to see what fits, as some of the ideas may fit your style and personality, while others may not. Most of all, have fun and enjoy the time you have with your kids, because someday, mom, you will have to let them go.

engage fantasy and fuel imagination

Young children are naturally creative and love to escape into the world of make-believe. Fantasy and imagination are a critical part of early childhood development, especially in today's society in which many children are being robbed of their childhood by being thrust into the adult world much too early.

When a mother embraces the imaginary world with her child, she often finds that a little imagination can result in a lot of co-operation. Young children respond positively when they see Mom enter their world. And remember, the world of make-believe is not just for preschoolers. School-age children also enjoy and benefit from imaginary play. When we stimulate and nurture children's imaginations, it's emotionally and intellectually satisfying as it allows them to use their creative abilities to enjoy the world around them. Simply put—it lets kids be kids.

Sugar Bugs

Most children do not get their teeth clean by brushing them themselves—but of course they *want* to do it all by themselves! You can talk to them about plaque and tooth decay, but they probably won't get it.

I don't believe in lying to children to motivate them, but we do need to communicate in language they understand. What they will understand is this: "Every day when you eat your food, you get sugar bugs on your teeth. When you brush your teeth, it makes the sugar bugs go away, but if you don't get them all, they will put holes in your teeth, and then your teeth will hurt. You are a big boy and can brush your teeth all by yourself, but Mommy needs to check to make sure you got rid of all the sugar bugs." So after

No More Tangles

When Teri was a little girl, her fine blond hair was always in knots. Trying to brush it was a nightmare for both of us—painful for her and challenging (sometimes draining) for me. I tried reasoning with her, explaining that the snarls would be impossible to get out if we didn't brush her hair every day. Once, I confess, I even tried brushing her hair while she was sleeping.

Then one day I pulled a chair into the bathroom, gave Teri a purse and a pair of high heels, and told her that she had an appointment in my beauty shop. Whenever we played beauty shop, Teri would patiently sit in the chair while I "styled" her hair and brushed out all the snarls.

your child brushes his teeth all by himself, you can then take his toothbrush and go over every tooth to make sure all the sugar bugs are gone. Trust me on this one—it works!

Cleanup Time

Picking up toys and doing chores can actually be fun! Here are some simple ideas:

- Tell your children they are elephants and need to pick up the toys with their trunks.
- Set the timer to see how fast your kids can pick up their toys. If the toys are picked up before the timer goes off, they get a treat.
- When your children are old enough to help you with cleaning the house, tell them it's time to play Cinderella. Let your kids dress in old, sloppy clothes while doing chores. When the chores are done, wash up, change clothes, and have a fancy lunch.

Indoor Tree House

When I was a little girl, I remember when my parents got a new refrigerator. The reason I remember this occasion has nothing to do with the refrigerator—in fact, I don't have a clue what it looked like. I remember it because my parents kept the box for a few days, and they let my sister and me use it for our private hideaway. We pretended it was our tree house.

Children love having their own private space where they can play. If you have room in your home for an indoor "tree house," leave it up for a few weeks until the novelty wears off. You can probably get an appliance box from your local appliance store, but another way to create a tree house is to put up a card table and cover it with a sheet or blanket. Let your kids keep a flashlight, some coloring books, and a few toys in the tree house, and they will enjoy many hours of fun.

A Trip to the Grocery Store

Let your kids go grocery shopping at home. Get out the nonbreakable food items such as pasta, pudding, and cake mixes from your pantry and set them out where your kids can reach them. Make a grocery list, use a small wagon for the grocery cart, and let your kids shop by putting the food items in the wagon. After they've collected the groceries, have them put the items in grocery bags and bring them back to the kitchen. Unpacking the groceries and putting the food in the pantry is part of the trip.

When the shopping trip is over, you'll have nothing to clean up!

Indoor Zoo

Gather all the stuffed animals together and let your kids create an indoor zoo. You can use boxes for the cages and small blankets or bath towels for areas where the animals can roam. Have your kids make tickets for the visitors, and someone certainly needs to be the zookeeper!

The Family Band

Create a family band by giving each person an "instrument." Old tennis racquets work well for guitars, and an upside-down plastic bowl with wooden spoons becomes an instant drum set. The lids to your pots and pans can be cymbals (if you can stand the noise!). Put on your favorite music and sing along while playing your instruments. You may want to get the video camera going for this one!

Role Reversals

For a few hours of hilarious fun, let your kids be the parents and you and your spouse be the children. It could be an eye-opening experience!

- At the dinner table, have the kids act as the adults, passing the food and telling the "kids" to eat their food. Mom and Dad can act as kids—swinging their legs or refusing to eat their peas!
- In the car (but of course the parent is behind the wheel!), Mom and Dad can act like kids by complaining about the boring trip ("Are we there yet?) while the kids try to offer creative ideas to pass the time.
- When it's time for some house cleaning, let the kids take charge and Mom can follow orders.

creativity in the kitchen

My kids were very picky eaters, and getting them to eat healthy food was always a challenge. Many of my attempts failed. I found out that tuna fish doesn't qualify as a pizza topping, and telling my kids that peas were power pellets didn't make them taste any better. But I did try a few things that worked, so maybe they will work for you.

Banana Men

Cut a banana in half and put it on a popsicle stick. Use a little cake icing from a tube to make eyes, a nose, a mouth, and a few strands of hair. Your kids will enjoy eating this healthy treat from the stick and may even want more than one.

Surprise Cup

For a great afternoon snack, fill a plastic mug with apple slices, carrot sticks, cheese cubes, raisins, and other healthy snacks. At the bottom of the cup, put two or three sweet treats such as chocolate chips, jelly beans, or M&M's. As your children eat the healthy snacks in the cup, they'll eventually find the surprise at the bottom.

Personal Pancakes

Transform a pancake into something exciting by simply extending the batter to make a couple of ears. Teddy bears, kitty cats, and puppy dogs can liven up your child's breakfast plate and get your

Guess Who's Coming to Dinner

Add some fun to your mealtime by setting an extra place at the table for one of your child's favorite dolls or stuffed animals. Be sure to include the special guest in your mealtime conversation. And if the special guest eats all of his food, he gets to have dessert too!

morning off to a happy start. You can use raisins for the eyes and a chewable vitamin for the nose. In the winter I made snowman pancakes by overlapping three small circles of batter. One morning, when I was in a rush and not in a creative mood, I made regular, boring, round pancakes. Rob was rather disappointed when I gave him his pancake. With a look of sadness in his eyes, he asked, "Why didn't you make a special pancake today?" I quickly replied, "It is a special pancake—it's a basketball!" His smile returned as he picked up his fork and ate his basketball.

Gingerbread Cookies

"Keep it simple!" is one of the rules I live by, and I found a very simple way to make gingerbread cookies using a gingerbread cake mix.

1 box (14 ounces) of gingerbread cake mix

¼ cup hot water

2 tablespoons flour

2 tablespoons margarine or butter, melted

In a medium bowl, mix all the ingredients together with a spoon until the dough forms a ball. Cover and refrigerate for 1 hour.

Occupy your children's attention and add to the fun by reading *The Gingerbread Man* while the dough is in the refrigerator.

Now divide the dough in half and place one half on a floured surface. Roll with a floured rolling pin until the dough is ¼-inch thick. Cut with floured gingerbread cookie cutters. Place cookies on an ungreased cookie sheet. Roll out the remaining dough and follow the same procedure.

Bake each pan of cookies 6–9 minutes in a preheated 375-degree oven.

Cool cookies for 1 minute before removing from the cookie sheet, and cool completely before decorating with frosting or candies.

Peanut Butter Balls

Fun to make and fun to eat!

2 cups natural peanut butter

½ cup honey (more or less to taste)

1 1/2 cups nonfat dry milk

½ cup coconut

½ cup raisins

½ cup sunflower seeds

Mix all the ingredients together and roll into balls. Place the balls on a cookie sheet and chill in the refrigerator for 2 hours. Makes around 30 balls.

Ants on a Log

For a healthy midday snack, take a celery stick, 4–5 inches long, and fill the crevice with peanut butter. Top with a few raisins, and it's ready to eat.

Homemade Butter

Pour a half-pint of whipping cream into a clear jar with a tight lid, and let your kids shake it up and down until it turns to butter. It takes a while, so be patient! When it finally turns to butter, spread it on a slice of their favorite bread or crackers.

Finding the Star

Hold a shiny red apple in your hand as you tell this story:

Once upon a time, there was a little boy who couldn't find his house.

"What does your house look like?" said a kind squirrel who wanted to help.

"Well," said the boy, "it's shiny and red, and it doesn't have any windows, but it has a star in the middle."

"Is this your house?" said the squirrel when he saw a shiny red apple.

"Yes, I think it is!" said the little boy.

"But where is the star?" asked the squirrel.

"Come inside and see!" said the little boy.

After you tell the story, cut the apple in half horizontally and show your child the star in the middle. Now slice the apple into bite-size pieces and eat it.

Cupcake Celebrations

One day when I picked up Teri from gymnastics, she told me how she'd performed a cartwheel on the balance beam.

"Wow! That's terrific!" I exclaimed as any proud mother would.

With a great sense of accomplishment, she added, "I think this calls for cupcakes!"

Cupcakes, you see, were sort of like a love language in our house. I've often made cupcakes to celebrate life's little pleasures as well as more significant events: the first day of school, the last day of school, a snow day (with school canceled), a rainy summer day. I could find a good reason to bake these treats almost any day!

So when the cake mixes went on sale at the grocery store, I always bought a healthy supply to keep my pantry well stocked. Cake mixes, I found, are easy to have on hand and whip up into dessert, and they provide a quick treat without having to go to the store or spend a lot of money. You can make them extra special with icing, whipped cream, or a dusting of powdered sugar, or you can eat them plain.

If, like me, you don't want your kids pigging out on junk food, freeze half of every batch of cupcakes (they thaw just fine), and pull out that other half to enjoy at a later date.

Formal Dining

If you have a formal dining room, don't just save it for special occasions or guests. Use it with your family at least once a week. Having meals in the dining room encourages good behavior and meaningful conversation. It removes your family from the clutter of the kitchen and provides an elegant setting.

Lighting candles and playing soft music can add to the ambiance. It is important to teach our children to be comfortable in formal settings so that they will develop good social skills and won't panic if they get asked to the junior prom. When your kids are old enough (leave the two-year-old with the babysitter), take them out

Cooking Lessons

When your kids are old enough to help in the kitchen, let each of them try their hand at cooking the meal.

- Let them help plan a menu—and write it out.
- Take them to the grocery store to get the ingredients they need.
- Savor the one-on-one time.

to a fancy restaurant with white linen tablecloths and multiple sets of silverware. Teach your children proper table manners and which fork to use for the salad. Going to a formal restaurant also requires proper attire. No blue jeans allowed. (Note: buy a book on manners if you need to learn a few things yourself—like most of us do!)

Informal Dining

Find or buy a plain plastic tablecloth you can use just for fun or for special occasions. Let it be something the kids can draw or write on with pen or marker. If friends are over, allow them to participate too. This will certainly become a tablecloth to keep and treasure for many years.

arts and crafts

Okay—this is where I'm really challenged! I am not an artsy-craftsy person, but teaching preschool for five years helped me learn some fun and easy activities for kids that I can pass along. The good thing about crafts is they can occupy your kids for hours. The bad thing about crafts is they can be messy.

Just make sure they do the messy stuff in the basement or outdoors rather than in the living room. Putting bath towels, newspapers, or plastic tablecloths on the kitchen counter, table, and floors can also protect your home and make cleanup a breeze.

Homemade Play Dough

1 cup flour

1 cup water

½ cup salt

2 teaspoons cream of tartar

1 tablespoon oil

5–6 drops food coloring

Mix all the ingredients together in a heavy pan over medium heat, and stir constantly until the mixture is thick and blended and your arm is ready to fall off. Knead a few minutes while it's still

Sibling Lunch

When Scott was in kindergarten, he attended classes in the afternoon. In the morning he and Teri usually played in the playroom until it was time for lunch. Rather than call them to the kitchen, I brought their lunches to the playroom and let them eat together on a blanket. I packed their food in lunch boxes so they felt like "big kids." It was easy for me and fun for them, and it's a memory they both cherish.

warm, and then it's ready to use. Rolling pins, cookie cutters, and plastic knives will keep your kids busy for hours. Store the play dough in airtight plastic bags or containers. It lasts for a long time, but you will want to make a new batch when it gets dirty.

Easy Costumes

For a fun and affordable costume (with no sewing required!), a paper grocery bag or an old pillowcase works great. Cut out a hole in the top for your child's head to go through and an arm hole on each side. You may also have to slit the front or back to make the costume fit better and go on more easily. Have your child color the paper bag or pillowcase with crayons or markers to create the costume he or she desires. There are tons of possibilities, but here are a few suggestions: firefighter, police officer, Pilgrim, Indian, ballerina, queen, king, or soldier. You can also make animal costumes, such as tigers, leopards, or dinosaurs, or vegetable costumes, like pumpkins or tomatoes. The costumes are easy to fold and store

A Pillow for School

Teri played tennis in high school and was also on the crew team. Since T-shirts are often printed and sold as money makers for the team, by the end of her senior year she owned almost enough T-shirts to open a T-shirt store. As we sorted through her drawers, she decided to pass a few down to her cousins, bring a few to college, and keep a few for memories. I surprised her by making a pillow for her dorm room from one of the "keepsake" T-shirts. She liked it so much she begged me to make a few more.

in a drawer or under the bed, and they can easily be replaced if lost or damaged.

Sock Puppets

When your kids' socks get holes in them, don't throw them away! Turn them into sock puppets by gluing or sewing on some eyes, a nose, and a mouth. If the socks are light in color, you can also make a face by using markers. Let your kids create a sock family and have a puppet show.

Aquarium

We tried having goldfish for a while, but guess who had to clean the stinky water and remember to feed them every day? And guess what happened when we returned from vacation—yep, they were floating belly-up on top of the water while my kids stared at them in horror. After we gave them a proper burial, we created an aquarium that was maintenance free. If this sounds like a good plan to you, here is what you need:

a shoe box (no lid)

blue and brown crayons, markers, or paint

orange construction paper

small seashells

thread

Have your child color or paint the inside of the shoebox blue (except one side of the box, which will become the "floor"). Color or paint the floor of the box brown to look like sand. Draw a few goldfish on the orange paper and cut them out. Set the shoebox on its side (with the brown floor at the bottom) and glue one or two fish to the back wall. Hang another fish or two from the top of the box with thread to give the aquarium a three-dimensional look. Glue sea shells on the floor and add anything else you wish to make the aquarium fun and interesting.

This One's a Keeper!

When Teri was five years old, we were shopping for school supplies shortly before her first day of kindergarten. She picked out a lunch box with a picture of a little girl that could have been her! The little girl's pink bib overalls, blond pixie haircut, and bright blue eyes made me think of Teri the moment we saw it. I was not surprised that this was the lunch box she wanted. After several years

of use, when it was covered with scratches and cracks, I asked Teri if I could finally throw it away. She responded in horror, "No, you can't throw that away! It's my childhood!"

T-Shirt Pillows

Save your kids' favorite T-shirts and turn them into pillows. Cut off the sleeves and sew up the neck and armholes—even moms with little or no sewing skills can do this! You can stuff the T-shirt with pillow stuffing or use the material to cover a pillow form. Let the kids help with this fun project, or keep it a secret and give the pillows to your kids as Christmas, birthday, or graduation presents.

Colorful Caterpillars

Cut an egg carton in half lengthwise so that you have two long sections with six "bumps" in a row. Have your child color the bumps and draw a face on the front. Use toothpicks or pipe cleaners for the antennae.

Spring Flowers

Start with a blue piece of construction paper. Take three cupcake papers and glue the bottom of each one to the blue paper so that they are arranged toward the top of the paper. Using a green crayon, draw a stem and some leaves for each of the flowers, and draw grass at the bottom of the paper. You can open up the flowers by pressing your hand to flatten the cupcake papers for a few seconds.

Thumbprint Critters

All you need is a set of watercolor paints, a piece of white or light-colored paper, and a small bowl of water. Have your child dip his or her thumb in the bowl of water, rub it on any color of paint, and press it onto the paper, making several thumbprints. When the paint is dry, he or she can use an ink pen or marker to draw eyes, a nose, ears, and whiskers on the thumbprints.

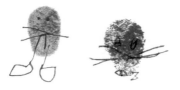

Snowman Pictures

You don't have to go out in the cold to make a snowman! To create a winter snow scene, you will need the following:

blue construction paper
white and black crayons
cotton balls
school glue

Pull apart the cotton balls slightly and glue them on the paper to create one or two snowmen. You can also glue some cotton on the bottom of the picture to make snow on the ground. Use a white crayon to draw snowflakes in the sky. Use a black crayon to make hats for the snowmen. With a fine-point marker you can also add eyes, noses, and mouths.

Alphabet Books

For a fun craft idea that is also educational, have your kids create their own alphabet books. Let your kids page through old magazines or mail-order catalogs (that you don't want anymore), and use them to find pictures for their books. Have them find a few items that begin with each letter of the alphabet, cut them out, and paste them onto pages of paper that you can staple or fasten together to make a book. You can also do this with colors or numbers.

memorabilia: what to keep, what to toss

One Christmas season when we were getting out our decorations and placing them around the house, I came across some things the kids had made in school. There was a nativity scene Teri had painted and some ornaments Rob and Scott had made.

As I set the picture on a shelf and hung the ornaments on the tree, Scott asked, "Why do you keep those things?"

Before I had a chance to answer, Rob replied, "Because it's good for our self-esteem!"

When your children go to school, they often come home with papers, ribbons, certificates, and works of art that can be very meaningful to you and to them. But unless your house is the size of the Hilton, you can't possibly save everything. So how do you know what to save and what to toss?

Here's what worked for me:

- If it was flat and eight inches by ten inches or less, it went into a scrapbook.
- If it was larger than eight by ten, or if it was not flat, it went into a box that each of my kids had in their bedrooms.
- If it was a work of art, it went on the refrigerator for a while before being transferred to the box.
- If it was a clay sculpture or figurine, it went on a shelf in the curio cabinet.
- If it was too big for the box (like the solar system Rob made for a science project), we'd put it on display for a while in a prominent place in the house. Eventually it would end up in the basement, where it remained until it was time for the trash. But before tossing it out, we'd take a picture of it and put the picture in a scrapbook or photo album.
- Go through the "keeper" boxes from time to time and discard things no longer sentimental or important to keep.

° Shortcuts °

When it comes to raising kids and creating memories, there are no shortcuts. Kids need our time, attention, and love. I realize that for many moms, however, this is a challenging task, as they may have outside responsibilities that rob them of valuable time they wish they could have with their children. The important thing, moms, is to make the most of the time you *do* have with your children and to create the kinds of memories you want your children to have. Maybe you can't read to your kids every night before they go to bed, but you *can* read to them every Sunday afternoon. Maybe you can't take them on a week's vacation for spring break, but you *can* take them for a bike ride on Saturday. Maybe you can't go camping for a weekend in the summer, but you and a friend *can* take your kids to the beach for an afternoon. Maybe you can't go to Disney World, but you *can* spend an evening riding roller coasters at the county fair. These small bits of time here and there can add up to a lifetime of positive memories for you and your children. And be sure to preserve those memories with a method that works for you.

build the future

The pressure of today's materialistic society makes raising a family very difficult. We used to have small houses and big families. Now we have big houses and small families. What used to be luxuries are now necessities. Many parents cannot make ends meet without two incomes—even if they are living modestly.

If you choose to make financial sacrifices in order to spend more time with your children, it is a decision you will never regret. Children are more important than possessions. When you come to the season of life when you have to let your children go, it won't matter what size house you lived in, how many cars were in your garage, or what kind of designer handbag you carried on your arm. What *will* matter is how much time you spent with your children and what you taught them about life.

Raising children is a ministry—and our kids are our mission field. As moms, we have the opportunity, responsibility, and privilege to train them up in the way they should go. One Sunday our pastor brought home this truth in a very powerful way. During his sermon on ministry, there were several moms on the platform behind him. One mother was rocking her child, another was playing with her child, while another was flipping through a picture book with her child. (I wondered if we had run out of room in the nursery!)

Our pastor spoke about the visible ministries we have, such as speaking, teaching, or being an elder or deacon in the church. He also spoke of behind-the-scenes ministries that are equally important—like greeting, hospitality, or working in the kitchen. Then he finally explained why the moms and children were behind him on the platform—to serve as a visual reminder that raising children is also a ministry. And if God has brought children into our homes, then raising them should be a top priority as we are called to love, nurture, and teach them.

Our pastor's words forever changed my attitude toward raising children. They also made me realize that if I raise God-fearing, honest, hardworking individuals, I am not only fulfilling my responsibility, I am also making a valuable contribution to society and the next generation.

Do you view motherhood as a ministry? If you do, it adds so much value and purpose to the task at hand. It can help on those days when the dishes are dirty, the laundry needs to be folded, and the kids spill Cheerios all over the floor.

Raising children is the hardest job you'll ever have to do. No one ever said it would be easy. And no one expects you to be a perfect mom because you *can't* be a perfect mom. But ask God to help you be a good one, and watch how he honors your request. He'll take all your imperfections and work through them as you build memories of being faithful every day, leaving your family with the best keepsake of all—a legacy of love and faithfulness.

notes

1. Crystal Bowman, *Cracks in the Sidewalk* (Grand Rapids: Baker, 2001), 72. Used by permission of Baker Publishing Group.

2. Carl Sandburg, quoted on www.brainyquote.com/quotes/quotes/c/carl sandbu107235.html.

3. Theodor Geisel, quoted on www.dr-seuss.com/dr_seuss_books_resources .html.

4. Crystal Bowman, *Meditations for Moms* (Grand Rapids: Baker, 2001), 32. Used by permission of Baker Publishing Group.

5. Ibid., 36. Used by permission of Baker Publishing Group.

index

accomplishments, 22, 30
acrostic poem, 35–36
adopted children, 31–33
Advent calendar, 59–60
alphabet books, 150
anniveraries, 80
aquarium, 145–46
arts and crafts, 142–50
autograph book, 92

baby pictures, 45
baby teeth, 23–24
bedside journal, 125
Bible, 41–42, 56, 76–77, 119–24
birth, of child, 44, 100–102
birthdays, 21, 49, 79
blessings, 105–7, 118

calendar, 19, 49
calendar journal, 81
camcorders, 65
charity, giving toward, 63–64
Charlie Brown Christmas, A, 64
childhood events, 44–45
child rearing, 127–30
chores, 133

Christmas, 49, 53–55, 58–70
  cards, 62–63
  dishes, 60
  movies, 64–65
  ornaments, 64
  tree, 60–61
colorful caterpillars, 147
computers, 49, 125
cookbook, 75
cooking, 136–41, 142
corn kernels, 56
costumes, 144

death, 29–30, 109
devotions, 76–77
diaries, 98–100
dining, 141–42
divorce, 29
Dobson, James, 70
dreams, 109–12

Easter, 70–72
electronic journals, 49
elementary school years, 46–48
emails, 49
experiences, creating, 40–41
extended family, 66–67

family album, 49
family band, 135
family devotions, 76–77
family nights, 72
fantasy, 131–35
Father's Day, 80
Focus on the Family, 70
food, 136–42

getaways, 58–59, 86–88
gingerbread cookies, 137–38
goals, 109–12
grandparents, 33–34, 78–80, 91
gratitude, 68
Greenwood, Barbara, 58
guest book, 95

high school years, 47–48
holidays, 51–81
    stress from, 68–70
homeschoolers, 20–21
hopes, 109–12

illness, 29
imagination, 131–35
individual attention, 89–90
indoor activities, 41, 133, 134–35
injuries, 23
inspiring moments, 108
interviews, 34

Jesus, birthday party for, 63
Joshua, 11
journaling, 13–49, 57
    persona, 97–100
    and prayer, 76, 115–19
    and Scripture, 119–24
    and stress relief, 102–5

keepsakes, 73, 148, 150–51

letter writing, journaling as, 16

mealtimes, 73, 137, 141–42, 143
meeting people, 93–94
memorabilia, 95, 150–51
Memorial Day, 72

memorials, 110
memories,
    creating, 10, 130, 152
    preserving, 10–12, 152
    recalling, 112–15
    worth of, 48
Metaxas, Eric, 58
middle school years, 47
milestone moments, 19
mission trips, 90–91
motherhood, as ministry, 153–54
Mother's Day, 80
movie camera, 65
moving, 26–28
multi-family vacations, 91–92

nativity, 62
note taking, 119–20
nursing homes, 65–66, 69

ornaments, 64

past, 112–15, 130
penmanship, 15
perfectionism, 15
photographs, 45, 95, 114
picnics, 41
poetry, 35–40
postcards, 95
prayer, 56, 75–76, 115–19
pregnancy and birth stories, 100–102
preschool years, 45–46
prose poem, 38–40

quality time, 87, 89
quiet time, 118
quote book, 14

Rainey, Barbara, 57
recipes, 75
rhyming poem, 36–38
role reversals, 135

school, 20
seasons of life, 44
secret pals, 77–78
secular celebration, 70–71

sharing journals, 42–43
shopping, 78–79, 134
Skarmeas, Nancy J., 58
snowman pictures, 147–48
sock puppets, 145
special occasion journal, 81
special place, for journaling, 57
spring flowers, 147–48
stepchildren, 33
stories, 73, 86
sugar bugs, 132–33
Sundays, 72, 73–74

teenagers, 28–29
Thanksgiving, 52–53, 56–58
thank-you notes, 67, 68
thumbprint critters, 149
time. *See* quality time
traditions, 53–80
tragedy, 29–31, 109
travel, 58–59, 71
tributes, 79–80
T-shirt pillows, 144, 147

vacations, 71, 83–95
Valentine's Day, 72, 77–78

This book evolved from **Crystal Bowman's** most popular workshops for mom-focused groups, including Hearts at Home and MOPS (Mothers of Preschoolers), both groups of which she is an active member.

As a lyricist, poet, author, speaker, former preschool teacher, and mother of three grown children, Crystal loves connecting with women and children. She's written and published more than thirty children's picture books, including books in the best-selling Little Blessing series, *My 1-2-3 Bible*, and *My Color Bible*; two books of humorous poetry (*Cracks in the Sidewalk* and *If Peas Could Taste Like Candy*); and a book of reflections for women (*Meditations for Moms*). In between it all, she writes lyrics for children's piano music and teacher-resource material.

When not making memories with her family or writing, Crystal is active in the local schools, often inspiring children with book readings (she's a member of the Michigan Reading Association) or teaching poetry in the classroom. She makes appearances on local television; is a frequent radio program featured guest; and speaks at literacy and writers conferences, women's retreats, and church events, offering sessions on journaling, parenting, and personal and spiritual growth.

Crystal and her husband divide their time between homes in Grand, Rapids, Michigan, and Florida.